STRATEGIC INVESTMENT APPROACH IN NON-BANKING FINANCIAL INSTITUTIONS

STRATEGIC INVESTMENT APPROACH IN NON-BANKING FINANCIAL INSTITUTIONS

A. Arulraj

G. Thiyagarajan

SERIALS PUBLICATIONS

NEW DELHI (INDIA)

First Published – 2009

ISBN: 978-81-8387-266-9

Published by

SERIALS PUBLICATIONS
4800/24, 1st Floor, Ansari Road
Darya Ganj, New Delhi-110002 (India)
Phone : 23245225. Fax : 91-11-23272135
E-mail: serials@satyam.net.in

Dedicated to

My Beloved Parents

T. Govindarajan & G. Sivakami

&

My Family

Dear Friend B. Raj Bahadur

&

Almighty Goddess Mariamman

finance charges have been kept low by the bank to gain market share. This has dented the growth of asset financing by the finance companies. Raising cost of operations, limited access to cheaper finance, stringent risk asset provisioning have taken toll on the asset finance companies. Diversification of risk through asset restructuring, sale of assets to asset managers and exploration of new business [illegible] management have reduced [illegible] leased assets [illegible] negative annual compounding growth.

Table [illegible]

CONTENTS

PREFACE

Non-banking financial system has been in existence from pre-independence days in India. From being practiced in an informal way, the non-banking financial players became more formalized financial units from 1940s. Till late sixties, the formal banking system was considered as credit delivery and scheme implementation agencies. In 1961, an attempt was made to bring the non-banking finance units into loose regulatory framework. The non-banking credit delivery gained importance in the late 70's and become more integrated into credit delivery mechanism in the late 80's. The Bhabatosh Datta Study Group (1971), James Raj Study Group (1975), Chakravarthy Committee (1987) and Narashimham Committee (1991) were the important committees to suggest transformation of unregulated non-banking financial sector into regulated one. The most notable of these committees is the Narashimham Committee which recommended for complete overhaul of existing regulatory framework for banking sector and bringing the non-banking finance sector into a systemic and tighter regulatory framework.

Reserve Bank of India prescribed tighter regulations to this sector as well. The aim of the regulatory framework was to safeguard the interests of the public, who invested sizable disposable income in these companies. Mandatory registration, fund raising linked to net owned funds & rating requirements, group and capital market exposure limits, liquidity maintenance norms, interest ceiling and prudential norms for income recognition and asset provisioning have transformed the non-banking finance companies into strong, vibrant and dynamic finance sector constituents. Recently, the classification of the non-bank finance companies has been revisited by the Reserve Bank of India. With the economic liberalization, globalization, the business profile of the Asset Finance Companies is transforming from fund-based activities to fee-based activities. Only few of the asset finance companies hold diversified business line. The riskiness of assets financed requires changing business perceptions. The global economic meltdown has created crunch for funds. It is against this backdrop, the attempt made in this book on understanding the changing business perceptions and mediating effects of performance is considered important

To comprehend the changing business profile of the asset finance companies under the stress of regulations, an attempt has been made to study the performance of the companies in post regulations. Though, there has been lot of research work on the regulatory effect of banking system, there is a few or almost neglible work in non-banking finance system. Raising many gaps in the existing literature on performance studies, the authors have conceptualized a model to understand the mediating effects of the performance of the asset finance companies. The comprehensive earnings, comprehensive expenses, business earnings profile and overall earnings are dimensions considered individually, the book concludes the cost is the mediating factor for successful businesses during inflationary conditions. However, the good investment strategy is to create more income opportunities and call for diversification into less risky fee-based activity. The ESW (NW)–PROFIT MODEL is considered as the best model that captures the determinants in designing appropriate investment strategy. The model will be helpful to the business executives, investors/stakeholders and consulting firms in making decisions in either funding or investing activities. The book is designed in a simple, coherent way so as to help the readers to comprehend and use the book in a better manner.

A. Arulraj
G. Thiyagarajan

1

NON-BANKING FINANCE SECTOR–A OVERVIEW

INTRODUCTION

The existence of the non-banking finance companies can be traced from pre-independence period but they were functioning in the unorganized sector. It was only in the late fifties, the non-banking finance companies were promoted in the organized sector. Although the Non-Banking Finance Companies (NBFCs) in India have survived for a long time but they shot into prominence only in the late 1980s (Ingres 2005). In the sixties, the reach of institutional financial intermediaries was quite limited. The magnitude of deposits with banks and NBFCs was of a small order to the tune of Rs.2, 494.80 Crores and Rs. 54.9 Crores respectively as on 31.3.1966. Inspite of operating for quite a long time in India, an attempt to regulate them started only in the sixties.

NON-BANKING FINANCE COMPANIES–A TRANSFOR MATION INTO REGULATED ENTITIES

In 1961, the NBFCs were brought into loose yet legalized regulatory framework from largely unregulated framework. The regulation of these institutions was found to be necessary for ensuring efficacy of credit and monetary policy, safeguarding depositors' interests and ensuring healthy growth of this sector (Vasudev 1998). The government constituted various committees to suggest the regulatory framework for the non-banking financial sector. The Bhabatosh Datta Study Group (1971), James Raj Study Group (1975), Chakravarthy Committee (1987) and Narashimham Committee (1991) were the important committees to suggest transformation of unregulated non-banking financial sector into regulated one. The inherent strengths of NBFCs such as high-level customer contact and satisfaction, geographical proximity, strong recovery mechanism were the drivers of their performance. Higher rates of interest on deposits offered by them afforded better opportunity of channelizing domestic savings into the financial markets (Ingres 2005). NBFCs had, practically, not been subjected to entry barriers, limitations on fixed assets and holding inventories in the form of gilt investments as they are now (Thiyagarajan, Arulraj 2005). Moreover, the NBFCs are in a consolidation phase now.

As the financial stability was threatened with many of the NBFCs offering unimaginable rates of interest of public deposits, their financial viability was adversely affected because of unrestricted lending even in the case of group exposure. The Narashimam committee on banking sector reforms (Narashimam 1991) suggested the guidelines for banking system should be extended to bring the non-banking finance companies within the ambit of an effective regulatory framework. Khanna Committee (Khanna P.R.1997) and Vasudev Committee (Vasudev 1998) have recommended exclusive regulatory framework for these companies such as mandatory registration, capital adequacy, linking of net owned funds[1] to deposits and application of prudential asset classification and income recognition norms. Non-Banking Financial Companies are reclassified broadly as Asset Finance Companies[2], Loan Companies and Investment Companies (Reserve Bank 2006).

With the application of the tighter regulations through Reserve Bank of India Directions 1998 (applicable to NBFCs), the advantages enjoyed by NBFCs *vis-à-vis* banks have eroded (Khan M.Y 2002). The purpose of the book is to focus on the trends in earnings and business profile on a macro level and to identify the factors affecting the performance of Asset Finance Companies (AFC, Equipment and Leasing NBFCs). Further from the literature, it is discernible that the NBFCs have started feeling the heat in the form of increased competition. In order to ward off the competition, they have been resorting to innovation in lending, diversification and exploration of new markets. From various studies published by the Reserve Bank of India (RBI), it is clear that the regulations have affected the financial strength of non-banking finance sector with many smaller finance companies have wound up their activities or merged with viable non-bank finance companies.

NON-BANKING FINANCE SECTOR–CURRENT SCENARIO

Non-Banking Financial Companies (NBFCs), especially the leasing and hire purchase companies, have recorded marked growth in recent years reflecting evolution of a vibrant, competitive and articulate financial system (Khan.M.Y.2003). Non-Banking Finance Companies are heterogeneous in their ownership patterns and regulations affect unevenly even within the broad category. Financial performance is impacted by regulations, competition and fund mobilization, deployment (Narasimhan.C.R.L.2006). The numbers of deposit taking Non-Banking Finance Companies are coming down as a result of erosion of investor's confidence, cost of operations (Narasimhan.C.R.L.2004). Contagion is less limited to non-banking financial sector than banking sector as far as its effect on economy is concerned in UK (Mathew Corder 2004). The restrictions on bank finance and group exposure will also have a marginally adverse impact on the resource profile of the Non-Banking Finance Companies (Krishnan Sitaraman 2007).

Banks have lower cost of funds than Non-Banking Finance Companies and the rising borrowing cost has resulted in contraction of their profitability. Asset Finance Companies' market share in truck financing has declined substantially, which has affected their business (Somasehar Vemuti 2007). The key drivers of performance of financial institutions are the riskiness of assets, demography and geographical spread and also affect the profitability (Krishnan Sitaraman 2004). Which are the drivers of performance of the financial institutions? Whether is it management strategy and its execution, environment (regulation, economy) that affects the performance? (Patrick T Harker, Stavros A Zenios.1998). Spreads are likely to reduce in capital market financing as a result of increasing competition (Megha Gupta 2007). There has been a significant shift in asset deployment away from the business of leasing, hire purchase towards loans, ICDs and investments. Overall cost of funds is higher for Non-Banking Finance Companies than for banks and returns have shrunk and operating cost have sharply increased resulting in closure of number of finance companies (Ingres 2005).

Delivery channels are crucial for cost and profit efficiency of financial institutions (Klumpes 2004). Operational reforms such as deregulation of bank finance, movement to loan financing have helped efficiency of the financial sector (Jayanth R Varma 2001). The asset turnoverability, return on funds deployed and return to investors is the useful guide to companies to decide about diversification or continuation (Amita S Kantawala 2004).

From the above and the industry publications, the problems[3] that these companies are facing today are

- Highly competitive asset financing environment
- Reduced return on lending
- Lack of business strategy to ward off competition.
- Economic factor viz., inflation, impacts the operations, and the performance.
- Regulations on income recognition, and prudential norms affect the earnings and profitability

REGULATORY EFFECT IN PERFORMANCE MEASUREMENT

It is essential to understand that the key drivers of performance of financial institutions; that are strategy, execution of strategy and environment and the firm's internal factors (Patrick T

Harker & Stavros A Zenios 1998). The performance of Non-Banking Financial Companies is influenced by the domestic profitability, asset management, and returns to scale (Amita S Kantawala 2004). In order to understand the cost efficiency and profit efficiency, it is essential to use non-parametric, econometric tools and avoid extensive use of accounting ratios (Robert DeYoung 2000).

Since the regulations have affected the performances of these companies, the understanding of the regulations and firm centric factors are quite demanding. These have compelled the companies to move from traditional business line (Khan M.Y. 2003). The share of the business of the asset finance companies has sharply came down with the deregulation of entry and banks entering in that business (Narasimhan.C.R.L 2004). The rising borrowing cost and declining lending rates have affected the business and profit margins (Krishnan Sitaraman 2007). But due to regulatory arbitrages, these companies can continue in their sphere of business (Somasehar Vemuti 2007). There is no comprehensive work to portray the business profile of these companies (Ingres 2005). Companies have diversified the product lines into consumer durables, used car finance, capital market financing yet their core profitability will be lower in the years to come.

With a robust credit appraisal, geographical proximity, strong risk management mechanisms and buoyancy in capital markets will ensure asset finance companies continued viability (Megha Gupta 2007). New business avenues that are opened up by the regulations such as credit card, asset management companies, insurance business are showing positive results. Companies having in-house subsidiaries are successful in improving business margins (Ingres 2005). Even the large-sized companies could not successfully manage the credit risks but the smaller ones can successfully manage it due to personalized service (Rakesh Mohan 2004).

Hence, in this book, the aim is to conceptualize various financial factors in evaluating the performance of asset finance companies. Very little empirical studies are done in this area, except use of financial ratios and absence of application of non-parametric tools, which require better understanding of key financial factors and implementation of a model to capture and evaluate it. The purpose of the book is to throw more light on the factors affecting the performance of the Asset Finance Companies that can guide the investors, lenders, company executives and other stakeholders to have a comprehensive knowledge of the functioning of these companies before investing their funds.

There is a dearth of integrated bank performance analyses that use an interdisciplinary and multivariate perspective. Bank performance analysis has been implemented commonly through budgeting, measuring total deposits, and branch profits; the latter two measures generate retrospective information which cannot be used to gauge the potential of a bank to generate retail banking business. Budgeting is criticised for placing too much emphasis on items that are outside the management's sphere of influence, and focusing on expense items rather than overall earnings (Smith III and Schweikart 1992).

In its widest sense, a firm's performance objective can be interpreted as maximising the value of its shareholders' investments at sustainable levels; thus, in the long term, the critical measure of overall bank performance should be business earnings (Gup, Fraser, and Kolari 1989). Hence, the concept of wealth maximisation is reviewed first. Hempel and Yawitz who have addressed the principle of equity value maximisation in the context of financial institutions, start off from the premise that "Wealth maximisation is the maximisation of the discounted cash benefits (earnings) to shareholders" (Hempel and Yawitz 1977). They, then, proceed to identify the key variables in cash benefits as gross receipts from assets, cost of liabilities, overhead costs, taxes, earnings are expected to be examined for the different ways they may interact with these key variables.

With measurement of overall performance in mind, they produce four categories of key variables influencing the equity value, namely, spread management, control of overhead, liquidity management, capital management, and net interest income, NII. These categories are explained in the works of Hempel and Yawitz (1977) and De Lucia et al. (1987). It involves lot of efforts to control the overhead costs or non-interest expenses, which deals with the ability of the bank to hold down such expenses even while maintaining a reasonable spread. It is not always true that control of overhead costs if business mix decisions for increasing the net interest income[4] are not closely scrutinised for their impact on earnings.

The constraint of containing the overhead costs is in the context of non-interest income (that is, fee income), constraint is defined as the net non-interest income (that is, difference between non-interest income and non-interest expenses). The accounting method decisions interact with other key firms decisions such as mix of business, financing, and operating decisions. The diversity in the accounting in the treatment of depreciation, deferred taxes, and provisioning may result in distortion of profitability than less diverse income recognition standards (Foster George 2002). The treatment of expenses such as research and development, pension, and many others seriously affect the comparability of the financial statements of the same company (Dawson 1975). From 1997, the companies are required to report the comprehensive income plus net income to reflect fairness in income recognition. Comprehensive income includes net income plus several comprehensive income items[5] in the income statement (Brigham Eugene 2004) & (RBI 1998).

VARIOUS DIMENSIONS IN MEASURING THE OVERALL PERFORMANCE OF NON-BANKING FINANCE COMPANIES EARNINGS COMPREHENSIVE NET INCOME (C-NI)

The following critical indicators of earnings have been identified as core to this criterion after consultation with previous research work, financial advisors, and industry executives: Regarding the earnings in the business, which includes core business income like lease rental, hire-purchase charges, non-core business income like other fee-based income such as consultancy fees, service charges and other fees,

Regarding the earnings from investing activities, which includes income in the form of dividend, interest on bonds, deposits, securities, income from the investment in subsidiaries and other non-business decisions.

COMPREHENSIVE EXPENSES (C-EXP)

The crucial indicators have been identified as essential under this criterion after consulting reputed auditors, tax consultants, and literature: Regarding the business expenses which are important for the operational and promotional activities; promotional activities include commission, advertisement and underwriting etc and operational activities include funding, staffing, and maintenance cost etc, Regarding the non-business expenses which are core to meet the riskiness of the assets through provisioning for non-performing assets, unrealized loss on sale of asset or securities marked-to-market, and other incidental recurring expenses such as audit fees, board expenses.

NET EARNINGS–NET PROFIT (NP)

The following core indicators have been identified under this criterion as critical success factors for the profitability; Regarding the operating profit from the operating activities, Regarding the non-operating profit from investing and funding activities which includes loans and advances to subsidiaries, investments in the issues of subsidiaries and other statutory requirements. According to the literature the profitability is affected by the increase in non-operational cost.

NON-PERFORMING ASSETS (NPA)

According to Reserve Bank of India, "a non-performing asset is an asset, in respect of which, interest has remained overdue for a period of six month or more. *NPA* includes term, demand or call loans, a bill, interest receivable from current assets and other loans, advances. It can be classified as substandard and loss asset" (Taxmann 2004). Substandard asset is an asset, which remained unpaid for more than 24 months, and loss asset is an asset, which remained unpaid for more than 36 months, which has been adversely affected by a potential threat of non-recoverability due to erosion in the value of security. Valuing *NPAs* is a difficult task and a *NPA* has a potential of wiping out entire earnings. However, the provisioning on the non-performing assets cushions the finance companies from reporting loss in future on this count.

In the third chapter, the authors have hypothesized various relationships among the variables in the conceptual model and mediating factors of the performance, income & cost on the various dimensions.

SALIENT FEATURES OF REGULATIONS IN ACTION IN NON- BANKING FINANCE SECTOR

Based on the recommendations of the Shah Committee (Shah 1992) and Vasudev Committee (Vasudev 1998), the Reserve Bank of India has brought in innumerable changes to the regulatory framework governing the Non-Banking Finance Companies (Reserve Bank 1998). It has put in place a comprehensive, consolidated new regulatory framework with the issue of directions applicable to these companies by the Reserve Bank of India (Taxmann 2004). The Reserve Bank of India amended the directions in 1999, 2000, 2003 (Taxmann 2004) and subsequently in 2006[6] (Reserve Bank 2006). The major salient features of the regulatory framework are:

The Non- Banking Finance Companies classification by the Reserve Bank is very objective oriented, i.e., the supervisory and control objectives (Khan 2003). He lists the classification of the NBFCs as below.

- Deposit-taking Non-Banking Financial Company-Company receiving deposits from public, institutions and corporate bodies

  Non-Deposit taking Non-Banking Financial Company-Company that does not receive deposits from general public, institutions and corporate bodies.
- Asset Finance Company-Asset Finance Companies are the non-banking finance companies, which primarily have business focus on equipment leasing, hire-purchase finance and whose lending to physical asset creation is at least 60% of its total assets.

- Loan Company–Financial Institution carrying on as its principal business the providing of finance whether by loans or advances or otherwise for any activity other than its own.
- Investment Company–Financial Institution carrying on as its principal business the acquisition of securities.

According to Rakesh Mohan, the linking of net owned funds (NOF), capital adequacy, and rating requirements are aimed at protecting the interests of the depositors. A NBFC can mobilize public deposit, if it is

- Company having NOF of less than Rs.2.5 million cannot accept any public deposit
- Company having NOF of Rs.2.5 million and above and complying with all prudential norms and having minimum investment grade rating can accept 400% of its NOF
- Company with NOF of Rs.2.5 million and above and complying with all prudential norms but not have minimum investment grade rating and have capital adequacy ratio of atleast 15% can accept 150% of NOF or Rs.10 Crore whichever is less (Rakesh Mohan 2004).

The inability of the non-banking finance companies to meet the liability of refunding the matured deposits forces us to suggest that all the Non-Banking Finance Companies shall maintain 15% of public deposits as statutory liquidity ratio in the form of approved securities not less than 10% and the remaining in unencumbered term deposits with commercial banks (Vasudev 1998).

The Non-Banking Finance Companies having public deposits of Rs.50 Crore and above on 31st March 2002 are required to submit returns on the exposure to capital market. With the stock market scam, the exposure of Non-Banking Finance Companies in the form of lending on equities, initial public offerings are severely restricted to protect the interests of the depositors (Ingres 2006).

As the lending of this sector is conditioned with uncertainty of recovery, the prudential norms prescribing the income recognition on the basis of provisioning requirements have put these companies on par with banks besides affecting the profitability due to non-performing assets norms (Kshisagar 2003). The equipment leasing and hire-purchase financing, which were major financing avenues have become less attractive and the non-banking finance companies have diversified their businesses into fee-based activities like consultancy, underwriting of public issues, and travel services (Crisil 2006). The relaxation of entry norms for undertaking insurance, asset management, has prompted non-banking finance companies with NOF of more than Rs.100 crores starting many joint ventures in insurance, which added substantial income to their businesses (Khan 2003). Regulations discriminate between deposit taking and non-deposit taking NBFCs. Even the deposit taking NBFCs are regulated in a less rigid sphere than banks. Available opportunity to NBFCs is regulatory arbitrage (Narashiman 2006).

EARNINGS PROFILE AND BUSINESS POTENTIALS OF FINANCIAL INSTITUTIONS

The hire-purchase finance companies in the non-bank finance sector are able to cover their interest charges due to high return on networth, earnings in this activity has considerably risen thanks to booming economy and consumers' favorable disposition in acquiring movable assets (Kantawala 2004). He used financial ratios to study the patterns and identify the key factors influencing the internal performance. Diversification and mergers, acquisitions is on the rise in the financial sector, some of them fail but many of them succeed and help the institutions to post decent and supernormal earnings (Jeon Bang 1997). The earnings of the non-banking financial institutions are mainly fund-based, i.e., lease income, hire-purchase charges, finance charges on personal loans, and fee-based income, i.e., underwriting commissions, consultancy, discounting charges etc. Traditionally, the fund-based income is the business earnings but recent trend is observed that there is a shift towards fee-based earnings, in which cost is substantially low. Earnings are a key input to augment capital required for supporting growth and absorbing business losses. Earnings also directly influence a company's ability to attract equity and debt (Crisil 2006). The earnings whether operational or adjusted for interest are significant irrespective of how the invested capital is measured. Invested capital may be measured as total or net operational assets or the share price or total market value: the results differ only very little. The operational earnings on invested capital based on the market values have little higher r^2 regressions (Tezel 2003). According to David Solomon, the economic profit is a measure of wealth creation "...as the difference between two quantities, net earnings and the cost of capital..." (Solomons 1965). Interest rate controls could worsen bank fragility by reducing bank earnings below the levels needed to sustain commercial viability. If lending to high risk borrowers is potentially profitable for banks, they would have incentives to evade the interest rate controls, using some other mechanism such as charging fees (Brownbridge 2000). The dominance of the multinational players, domestic institutions like ICICI has increased due to their advantages of competitive funding costs, support of international parents and sophisticated mechanisms to monitor and control risks. The stiff competition has forced the non-bank finance companies to change their business strategies like shift from traditional fund-based activities to fee-based activities and diversification into new businesses. The change in business strategies has, altogether, affected the earnings in core business sector (Ingres 2006). The severe squeeze experienced by finance companies on their operating as well as net margins can be attributed to high cost of debt, increase in operating expenses, low productivity and slow absorption of technology. In the financial services industry, Internet banking is already causing dents in conventional banking. The financial services industry is undergoing major transformation in business. The future opportunities will be in rural markets, fund-based activities–financing intangibles such as education, health, travel etc, and the fee-based activities in information technology, infrastructure, and environment sectors (Kshirsagar 2003). In order to understand the potential interaction between bank and non-bank markets, an important distinction relates to the separate influences of supply and demand factors. But there is an identification issue: observed changes in corporate bank and non-bank finance will reflect movements in both the supply of and demand for external funds and it is difficult to disentangle the two (Ursel Baumann 2005). Lending to micro-finance sector, viz., self-help groups is much more profitable and lowers the scope of the risk provisioning. The finance companies, through micro-finance, can increase their earnings (Ananth Bindu 2004). Reflecting the imperatives of the evolution of a vibrant, competitive and articulate a financial system, the NBF Sector in India has recorded marked development in the recent years in terms of number of NBFCs (Khan 2003).

CONCLUSION

The transformation of the non-banking finance sector from largely unregulated into highly regulated has forced many in the sector to opt for mergers. Regulations affected their casual fund raising attitude to a systemic and scientific ability to service the funds raised. The Central Bank's (Reserve Bank of India) measures on bringing the Non-Banking Finance sector to a regulated framework can be seen as a reactionary step to stop the finance companies from exploiting the weakness of the unregulated setup. The consolidation witnessed in the finance sector is due to the active role of the Reserve Bank in regulating the sector and safeguarding public money. The positive role played by the regulations has shielded the Indian Non-Banking Finance Sector from failing in the midst of recent failure of large of finance companies globally and global liquidity crisis.

NOTES

1. Net owned funds is equal to paid equity capital plus free reserves less accumulated loss balance, deferred revenue expenditure, other tangible assets (A) less investment in group, subsidiaries and in the sector and also book value of debentures, bonds, outstanding loans and advances with subsidiaries and group companies (B) (amount in excess of 10% of A).

2. Asset Finance Companies are the non-banking finance companies, which primarily has business focus on equipment leasing, hire-purchase finance and whose lending to physical asset creation is at least 60% of its total assets.
3. Refer various publications of the Equipment Leasing and Hire Purchase Association of India, industry comments contained in the publications of Ingres of Investment and Credit Rating Agency of India and Reserve Bank of India.
4. Net interest income is the difference between the interest income and interest expense. The interest spread is calculated on the net interest income.
5. Examples of the Comprehensive income items are unrealized gain or loss on sale of securities marked-to-market.
6. Reserve Bank of India has amended the classification of Non-Banking Finance Companies vide its circular issued by Department of NBS dated 6.12.2006.

2

FINANCIAL INSTITUTIONS– EARNINGS, RISK MANAGEMENT AND APPROACHES TO PERFORMANCE MEASUREMENT

INTRODUCTION

This chapter has sections that provide a comprehensive analysis of the research works pertaining to macroeconomic variables and corporate earnings, regulatory framework, studies on drivers of performance of financial institutions, financial services, performance measurement approaches like key financial ratios as performance measures, shareholders' wealth, dimensions measuring cost control and earnings.

TRENDS IN EARNINGS OF FINANCIAL INSTITUTIONS

The hire-purchase finance companies in the non-bank finance sector are able to cover their interest charges due to high return on networth, earnings in this activity has considerably risen thanks to booming economy and consumers' favorable disposition in acquiring movable assets (Kantawala 2004). He used financial ratios to study the patterns and identify the key factors influencing the internal performance. Diversification and mergers, acquisitions is on the rise in the financial sector, some of them fail but many of them succeed and help the institutions to post decent and supernormal earnings (Jeon Bang 1997). The earnings of the non-banking financial institutions are mainly fund-based, i.e., lease income, hire-purchase charges, finance charges on personal loans, and fee-based income, i.e., underwriting commissions, consultancy, discounting charges etc. Traditionally, the fund-based income is the business earnings but recent trend is observed that there is shift towards fee-based earnings, in which cost is substantially low. Earnings are a key input to augment capital required for supporting growth and absorbing business losses. Earnings also directly influence a company's ability to attract equity and debt (Crisil 2006). The earnings whether operational or adjusted for interest are significant irrespective of how the invested capital is measured. Invested capital may be measured as total or net operational assets or the share price or total market value: the results differ only very little. The operational earnings on invested capital based on the market values have little higher r^2 regressions (Tezel 2003). According to David Solomon, the economic profit is a measure of wealth creation "...as the difference between two quantities, net earnings and the cost of capital..." (Solomons 1965). Interest rate controls could worsen bank fragility by reducing bank earnings below the levels needed to sustain commercial viability. If lending to high risk borrowers is potentially profitable for banks, they would have incentives to evade the interest rate controls, using some other mechanism such as charging fees (Brownbridge 2000). The dominance of the multinational players, domestic institutions like ICICI has increased due to their advantages of competitive funding costs, support of international parents and sophisticated mechanisms to monitor and control risks. The stiff competition has forced the non-bank finance companies to change their business strategies like shift from traditional fund-based activities to fee-based activities and diversification into new businesses. The change in business strategies has, altogether, affected the earnings in core business sector (Ingres 2006). The severe squeeze experienced by finance companies on their operating as well as net margins can be attributed to high cost of debt, increase in operating expenses, low productivity and slow absorption of technology. In the financial services industry, Internet banking is already causing dents in conventional banking. The financial services industry is undergoing major transformation in business. The future opportunities will be in rural markets, fund-based activities–financing intangibles such as education, health, travel etc, and the fee-based activities in information technology, infrastructure, and environment sectors (Kshirsagar 2003). In order to understand the potential interaction between bank and non-bank markets, an important distinction relates to the separate influences of supply and demand factors. But there is an identification issue: observed changes in corporate bank and non-bank finance will reflect movements in both the supply of and demand for external funds and it is difficult to disentangle the two (Ursel Baumann 2005). Lending to micro-finance sector, viz., self-help groups is much more profitable and lowers the scope of the risk provisioning. The finance companies, through micro-finance, can increase their earnings (Ananth Bindu 2004). Reflecting the imperatives of the evolution of a vibrant, competitive and articulate a financial system, the NBF Sector in India has recorded marked development in the recent years in terms of number of NBFCs (Khan 2003).

MACROECONOMY AND CORPORATE EARNINGS

According to many researchers, strong Gross Domestic Product growth, a measure of economic growth, leads to sustained growth in many sectors finance being one of the sectors. The GDP is positively correlated to the dependent variables viz., earnings, returns to investors etc, which rejects the early research that GDP could not be a better indicator of economic well-being. We confirm that the GDP growth influences the earnings of the Non Banking Finance Companies in a significant way. Lower GDP does not mean higher earnings; the results only suggest that the GDP should not show divergence over the period (Thiyagarajan 2004a). Using a simple variant of widely-cited financial sector models, the effects of monetary policy on the profits of commercial banks. The primary contribution may well lie in suggesting the need and feasibility, as well as some of the difficulties, of relating banking industry profitability to the instruments of monetary control. Certainly, the banking profits are affected by the manner in which a given rate of growth in the money supply is implemented (Greenbaum 1976). Networth is the surplus of the assets over the liabilities. Alternatively, net worth is the amount of equity capital-paid up plus reserves and surplus. Networth of a company reflects the increase of the worthiness of investors' supplied capital over a period. The networth is strongly and positively influenced by the GDP (Thiyagarajan 2004b). According to Lo, "...the economic prosperity and low inflation will give a push effect to the economic units viz., private and public sector units and translates in the growth of profits and in other financial measures..." (Lo, Andrew 1984). The vast majority of economic news that is reported by the analysts is done on a current dollar or "nominal" basis. The implicit deflator measure inflation across all sectors of the economy and is the ratio of nominal to real (chain-weighted) GDP. The recognition of the substitution bias has led the fixed weighted deflator to be given the less attention than others (Mikolich 2004).

Economic growth can come from technological change and either from reinvesting earnings into existing firms, or the infusion of cash into new firms. Historically, much of economic growth has come from the infusion of cash into new firms, which does result in a higher growth rate of dividends per share for existing firms. Economic growth does result in a higher standard of living for consumers, but does not have direct bearing on growth in dividends (Ritter Jay 2003). Economic prosperity has created demand for consumer durables in India. Therefore, the opportunities for finance companies are plenty. Besides, the automobile production is driven largely by domestic savings, interest rate, inflation, and tax moderation. (Sharma 2005). Macroeconomic growth measured in terms of GDP or GNP might lead to increased bonuses, wages, and/or dividends. It, therefore, increases the costs and benefits for the stakeholders of the company. Safely, if there were no acceptable explanations that there is no corresponding increase in return when economy prospers, the shareholders would need to be told how the company intended to handle the loss of competitiveness (Oxelheim 2003).

The common feature of the economic theories is that there is an informational friction whose severity is endogenous. Given this feature, an increase in the rate of inflation drives down the real rate of return not just on money, but also on assets in general. The implied reduction in real returns exacerbates credit market frictions (Boyd J 2000).

CATEGORISATION OF NON-BANKING FINANCE COMPANIES

Based on the recommendations of the Shah Committee (Shah 1992) and Vasudev Committee (Vasudev 1998), the Reserve Bank of India has brought in innumerable changes to the regulatory framework governing the Non-Banking Finance Companies (Reserve Bank 1998). It has put in place a comprehensive, consolidated new regulatory framework with the issue of directions applicable to these companies by the Reserve Bank of India (Taxmann 2004). The Reserve Bank of India amended the directions in 1999, 2000, 2003 (Taxmann 2004) and subsequently in 2006[1] (Reserve Bank 2006). The major salient features of the regulatory framework are:

The Non- Banking Finance Companies classification by the Reserve Bank is very objective oriented, i.e., the supervisory and control objectives (Khan 2003). He lists the classification of the NBFCs as below.

- Deposit-taking Non-Banking Financial Company-Company receiving deposits from public, institutions and corporate bodies

  Non-Deposit taking Non-Banking Financial Company-Company that does not receive deposits from general public, institutions and corporate bodies.
- Asset Finance Company-Asset Finance Companies are the non-banking finance companies, which primarily have business focus on equipment leasing, hire-purchase finance and whose lending to physical asset creation is at least 60% of its total assets.

- Loan Company–Financial Institution carrying on as its principal business the providing of finance whether by loans or advances or otherwise for any activity other than its own.
- Investment Company–Financial Institution carrying on as its principal business the acquisition of securities.

According to Rakesh Mohan, the linking of net owned funds (NOF), capital adequacy, and rating requirements are aimed at protecting the interests of the depositors. A NBFC can mobilize public deposit, if it is

- Company having NOF of less than Rs. 2.5 million cannot accept any public deposit
- Company having NOF of Rs. 2.5 million and above and complying with all prudential norms and having minimum investment grade rating can accept 400% of its NOF
- Company with NOF of Rs. 2.5 million and above and complying with all prudential norms but not have minimum investment grade rating and have capital adequacy ratio of atleast 15% can accept 150% of NOF or Rs. 10 Crore whichever is less (Rakesh Mohan 2004).

The inability of the non-banking finance companies to meet the liability of refunding the matured deposits forces us to suggest that all the Non-Banking Finance Companies shall maintain 15% of public deposits as statutory liquidity ratio in the form of approved securities not less than 10% and the remaining in unencumbered term deposits with commercial banks (Vasudev 1998).

The Non-Banking Finance Companies having public deposits of Rs.50 Crore and above on 31st March 2002 are required to submit returns on the exposure to capital market. With the stock market scam, the exposure of Non-Banking Finance Companies in the form of lending on equities, initial public offerings are severely restricted to protect the interests of the depositors (Ingres 2006).

As the lending of this sector is conditioned with uncertainty of recovery, the prudential norms prescribing the income recognition on the basis of provisioning requirements have put these companies on par with banks besides affecting the profitability due to non-performing assets norms (Kshisagar 2003). The equipment leasing and hire-purchase financing, which were major financing avenues have become less attractive and the non-banking finance companies have diversified their businesses into fee-based activities like consultancy, underwriting of public issues, and travel services (Crisil 2006). The relaxation of entry norms for undertaking insurance, asset management, has prompted non-banking finance companies with NOF of more than Rs.100 crores starting many joint ventures in insurance, which added substantial income to their businesses (Khan 2003). Regulations discriminate between deposit taking and non-deposit taking NBFCs. Even the deposit taking NBFCs are regulated in a less rigid sphere than banks. Available opportunity to NBFCs is regulatory arbitrage (Narashiman 2006).

DIVERGING PRACTICES IN MEASURING FINANCIAL PERFORMANCE FINANCIAL RATIOS APPROACH TO PERFORMANCE MEASUREMENT

According to Fraser and Fraser (1990), and as indicated by the review of conceptual frameworks, the most commonly used financial ratios are those of ROE and ROA. The link between ROE and ROA is the equity multiplier as shown below:

ROA (Net Income/Average Assets) x EM (Average Assets/ Average Equity) = ROE (Net Income/Average Equity)

In essence, ROA is a measure of bank's profitability, EM is a measure of risk, and ROE is a summary measure of bank performance. According to Sinkey, the best measures of a firm's overall performance are the profitability ratios ROE and ROA (Sinkey 1983, p.201). Although the words, performance and profitability are sometimes used interchangeably as above, profitability ratios can be separated from risk ratios; in turn, profitability is represented under overall performance. Following table reviews key financial ratios on profitability overall performance.

Table 1
Key Financial Ratios to Measure Performance

Profitability Ratios
Net Income/Average Assets (ROA)
Net Interest Income/Average Assets
Non-Interest Income/Average Assets
Overhead Expense/Average Assets
Provisions for NPA/Average Assets
Interest Income/Average Assets
Interest Expense/Average Assets
Other Operating Expense/Average Assets
Staffing Expense/Average Assets
Summary Ratio (Overall Performance) = Net Income/Average Equity (ROE)

Thygerson stated that "...little academic research has been done on the subject of bank profitability [performance]" (Thygerson 1991, p. 19). The assertion of Thygerson is true inspite of many researchers attempted at arriving an overall performance model. Existing literature on measuring performance is dominated by reports of practitioners in the field or consultants, and the common denominator of these reports is management accounting. On the other hand, academic research is generally characterised by the development of econometric models, comprised of the multiple regression studies.

According to Kantawala, the ANOVA along with the details about average ratios may become a useful guide to companies to decide about diversification or continuation in the same line of business considering profitability within the regulatory framework (Kantawala S Amita 2004). He used 19 ratios in the study and profitability; asset utilization, turnover and return to investors are the dimensions that are explored in that study. The literature on stock predictability has evolved considerably over the last 20 years. Initial tests produced strong evidence that market returns are predictable, but subsequent research has argued that small-sample biases explain the bulk of apparent predictability. The accumulated evidence suggests that Dividend Yield, Book–to-Market Value Ratio, and Earnings-Price have, at best, weak power to predict returns

(Lewellen Jonathan 2002). A bank's operating performance is frequently measured using accounting ratios such as return on assets and return on investment. These ratios provide a great deal of information about a bank's financial performance compared with prior periods and compared with other banks' performance. Nevertheless, there are limitations to the use of these ratios. One is that financial ratios fail to consider the value of management's actions and investment decisions that will affect future as opposed to current performance (Sherman, Franklin Gold 1985).

A linear regression of an accounting measure of profit rate on the fraction of shares owned by the five largest shareholding interests and on a set of control variables, in which ownership structure is treated as an endogenous variable, gives no evidence of a relation between profit rate and ownership concentration. In attempting to assess the effect of ownership structure on firm performance, is it more sensible to look at an estimate of what management has accomplished or at an estimate of what management will accomplish? The second difference is in who is actually measuring performance. For the accounting profit rate, this is the accountant constrained by standards set by his profession (Demsetz, Villalonga 2001). According to Harker and Zenios (1998), financial performance of an institution–observable but non-actionable–can be affected by its performance along the axis of service delivery and financial intermediation. They concluded that the drivers of performance can be classified into, strategy, execution of strategy and the environment. Further, they felt diversified institutions benefit from opportunities for internal resource allocation and, therefore, can hold less capital and do more lending than more focused institutions. From the environment angle, they felt that drivers are innovation, regulations and technology (Information Technology).

In comparing bank performance among banks from different countries, especially across developed and developing countries, considerable care must be taken to allow for differences in product mix, capital structure, accounting conventions and especially inflation rates before drawing firm conclustions (Vittas Dimitri 1991). The financial sector reforms in India have significantly enhanced the productivity (performance) of private banks vis-à-vis public sector banks. Total assets and total credit advanced have grown. Additionally, the foreign banks outperform Indian private banks, and overall competitiveness has improved. Finally, the findings are increased competition has had a stronger positive effect on the productivity of domestic banks than on foreign banks. The variables included in the study were diversification measure, size, share of non-interest expenditure, and the profit (Sanyal Paroma & Shankar Rashmi 2005).

The cross-country empirical evidence for Asia suggests that the limited openness necessarily results in slower institutional development, greater fragility and higher costs of financial services. World-over, the financial services industry has made tremendous progress following the supply-leading approach[2] (Nisture Rupa Rege 2001). Turnover Index based on the financial products is found to be reliable to assess the state of financial services in the Indian economy. The index could be used as an indicator of performance of a particular company against the performance of industry or economy (Mohanty and others 2003). Economic Value Added (*EVA*) is an useful measure for assessing the performance so as to arrive at executive compensation. But Refined Economic Value Added (*REVA*) is a more appropriate performance measure from the investors' viewpoint (Bacidore Jeffrey, Boquist John and others 1997). *EVA*[3], the difference after-tax operating profits and the total cost of capital is promoted as a measure of a company's real profitability, and it is the only performance measure that ties directly to a stock's intrinsic value (Stewart 1991).

Credit Rating is a good measure of performance and that reflects the ability of the companies to meet the contingencies. However, rating alone is insufficient to address the issue. Therefore, capital adequacy can be a better measure of performance together (Altman, Saunders 2000). Non-Banking Financial Institutions in United Kingdom, have also received growing attention as banks since the adoption of audit and disclosure standards. The regulations have strengthened the muscles of the banks and institutions, in which sector there were lot of failures in nineteenth century in Britain. Hence, the achievement of financial standards could be performance measure (Barth, Caprio and Levine 2001). The market value added is significantly and positively associated with both the return on net operating assets and growth even after considering the effect of stock returns on the market value multipliers. Therefore, the accounting returns are preferable measures than residual returns (Tezel Ahmet 2003).

SHAREHOLDERS' WEALTH AS PERFORMANCE MEASURING VARIABLE

Literatures on financial management invariably cite the primary objective of corporate decision-making as maximising the shareholders' wealth (networth[4]) or market value of the firm to its shareholders (Aragon 1989; Bruce et al. 1991; Van Horne and Wachowicz 1995; Weston and Copeland 1992). Furthermore, the concept of maximising the equity value either historical or marketable, is not confined to academe. It is almost religiously quoted by chairpersons and managing directors in annual reports. In Kooken's words, "Increasing shareholder value has become the explicit goal of senior management..." (Kooken 1989, p.15). It is essentially an acknowledgment of management's accountability to shareholders, where agency costs can be minimised, and scarce resources allocated efficiently and effectively.

Hempel and Yawitz who have addressed the principle of shareholders' return maximisation in the context of financial institutions, start off from the premise that "Wealth maximisation is the maximisation of the discounted cash benefits to shareholders" (Hempel and Yawitz 1977, p.20). They then proceed to identify the key variables in cash benefits as gross receipts from assets, cost of liabilities, overhead costs, taxes, and appropriate risk premium to be added onto the risk-free interest rate; managerial decisions are expected to be examined for the different ways they may interact with these key variables.

While emphasizing the need to remember the principle of maximising shareholders' wealth in all decisions, Hempel and Yawitz (1977) also underscore the need for focusing this principle for the benefit of day-to-day decision-making. With the latter need in mind, they produce four categories of key variables influencing the equity value, namely, spread management, control of overhead, liquidity management, and capital management. These categories are briefly explained next with the help of Hempel and Yawitz (1977) and De Lucia *et al.* (1987).

Spread management refers to management of the difference between gross revenues and interest expenses. Although it is possible to realise high spreads in the short-run by mixing short-term liabilities with long-term assets, a more desirable state of affairs is to sustain a high positive spread over time within prudential supervision.

Control of overhead costs or non-interest expenses deals with the ability of the bank to hold down such expenses while maintaining a high spread. High gross spreads may not always translate into high net spreads if investment decisions are not closely scrutinised for their impact on non-interest expenses.

Liquidity management demands the presence of short-term assets that can be quickly converted to cash to meet unexpected deposit withdrawals or funding needs, and liquidity requirements of the Supervising Bank. Interest rates and monetary growth within the economy have to be monitored as part of this process. The bank management will attempt to hold enough short-term assets to meet anticipated liquidity requirements, without unnecessarily lowering the profit performance due to the generally lower yields associated with such assets.

Capital management refers to balancing the level of capital in such a manner that growth of assets and liabilities is sustainable without eroding public confidence or profitability. Sinkey (1992) uses Hempel and Yawitz's (1977) framework to arrive at a similar conceptual framework. The bank's primary objective of maximising shareholders' wealth is depicted as being shaped by owners' preferences, management's attitudes and decisions, and society; also listed are six policy strategies to achieve that objective. Management's attitudes and decisions, the regulatory and economic environment, and the objective of maximising investors' wealth (shareholders), in turn, influence these policies. The success of these policy strategies depends on the riskiness of a bank's balance sheet, that is, the nature of assets and the concentration of loan portfolios (Sinkey 1992). The primary objective of the board is to increase the realizable value of the equity whether on liquidation or through trading. The market value is conditioned by many factors viz., endogenous factors, namely, management attitudes, strategies, long-term business prospects and quality of assets and exogenous factors such as political, socio-economic environment and/or external shocks, therefore is subject to volatility (Kantawala 2004). The book value is conditioned primarily by the endogenous factors such as profit generated, management attitude to share the wealth of the company with the shareholders and is more likely to stay stable. Further it is based on historical cost. Therefore, the increase in book value could be a best indicator of performance (Khan M.Y 2003).

Large block holdings are not homogenous and we therefore distinguish between types of shareholdings. Insider control by families may be more efficient as ownership is in the hands of principals. They might feel more committed to the firm than outside agents such as financial institutions, which might take into account interests other than maximizing shareholder value, especially if they also have large credit arrangements with the firm (Gebhardt Günther 2001). The size effect focuses on management's tendency to engage in an over acquisitive program. However, there are countervailing considerations that might lead management to pursue an under acquisitive program. The action of management ends in loss of wealth of shareholders. This, again, triggers the shareholders' to look for maximization of their wealth, and to demand value creation (Linda Allen 1991). The meta-analytic findings suggest that corporate virtue in the form of social responsibility and, to a lesser extent, environmental responsibility is likely to pay off, although the operationalizations of Corporate Social Performance (CSP) and Corporate Financial Performance (CFP) also moderate the positive association. For example, CSP appears to be more highly correlated with accounting-based measures of CFP than with market-based indicators, and CSP reputation indices are more highly correlated with CFP than are other indicators of CSP (Marc Orlitzky 2003). The California Public Employees' Retirement System (CalPERS) was a leader in this wave of activism. Their study investigated the long-term returns an investor with public information could earn by buying a portfolio of firms targeted by CalPERS and whether the success of CalPERS' activism depends on the aggressiveness of the targeting. The evidence supports the idea that visible and aggressive activism leads to substantial increases in shareholder wealth while a quieter activism does not (Crutchley, Hudson, and Jensen 1998). Therefore, the measure of shareholders' wealth plays a crucial role in assessing the performance. Much literature surveyed, uses either Market Value Added (*MVA*)[5] or Economic Value Added (*EVA*) to assess the performance of a company. They ignore, the important fact that not all the companies in the financial sector are listed, and/or actively traded. This is a peculiar situation in emerging and underdeveloped market economies (Brigham 2002).

SUCCESSFUL COST CONTROL STRATEGIES FOR FINANCIAL INSTITUTIONS

The cost of funds for financial institutions, particularly the non-banking finance companies, rose to an unimaginable level and affected the profitability of these institutions. The rise in funding cost can be attributed to the high inflation, economic growth, dramatic rise in consumption finance, and credit risk associated with (Rakesh Mohan 2004). Though a firm's total cost of capital also depends on its cost of debt, the cost of debt depends in subtle ways on how a firm is taxed. The focus on the cost of equity capital avoids dealing with complicated taxation issues. With the relaxation of foreign investment in financial sector, the cost of financing is coming down and the avenues to raise the funds are increasing (Stulz 1999). The Data Envelopment Approach is useful to estimate the efficiency score for financial institutions and to identify the key costs necessary and overspent areas (Berger Allen 1997). The social costs weighs more than corporate financial costs, nowadays. The society expects the financial institutions to spend substantial earnings towards the society in the form of welfare measures (Orlitzky Marc 2003).

The financing cost can be brought down, if the banks and financial institutions raise the internal accruals through more retention of earnings. It is the cheapest source of finance, not costless given the opportunity cost (George Foster 2002). The restrictions on commissions for agents, and regulation on advertising has affected the access to public deposits. Therefore, the cost of finance has increased and the profitability has fallen significantly. Additionallly, the restriction on access to bank finance through exposure norms has put strains on cost control (Bansal 1994). General proposition is that regulation imposes additional cost on the units but it is also helpful in increasing the efficiency. A similar result applies to mergers and acquisitions: some consolidations improve cost efficiency, whereas others worsen the performance of the combined institution relative to the separate institutions (Barth James 2001). The effectiveness of the cost control strategies may be reflected in rise in profits in the immediate future. But efficient control of cost can be measured using parametric and non-parametric tools such as Data Envelopment Analysis (*DEA*), Fourier Frontier Analysis, and Generalized Autoregressive Conditional Hypothesis (*GARCH*) etc (Gujarati 2004). The firms' choice between several possible combinations of labour and capital costs, and choose those, which minimize the costs, and thus maximize their profits. The cost of the capital was generally higher for the private companies than for the one-man businesses or the public companies. Staffing cost, administrative cost that can be controlled is on the rise due to trends in intra-industry and inter-industry (Khan 2002). NBFCs are heterogeneous in their ownership patterns (such as foreign or domestic) and in the nature of activities undertaken.

Regulations affect unevenly even within the broad category. Hence, there is no level playing field not only between NBFCs and banks but also between NBFCs themselves (Narashiman 2006).

APPROACHES TO RISK MANAGEMENT IN FINANCIAL INSTITUTIONS

According to Eugene, "Risk is a systematic uncertainty of outcome. Risk can be classified as financing or credit risk, market risk, and management or operational risk" (Brigham 2004). Measuring and managing credit risk has become core for financial institutions. In most countries, banks' equity requirements are already tied to their exposure to credit risk. (Dangl 2003). Financing or Credit risk is of paramount importance for investment decisions. Credit risk exposure, when exceeds the networth, then the financial institutions will face erosion of funds. The prudential norms on provisioning and income recognition will take care of that (Mohan Rakesh 2004). Schmit presented the first empirical results on the default and loss severity of leases by implementing a non-parametric simulation based on ex ante and ex post data on four types of leases. He felt that there is an urgent need to review the capital adequacy proposals in order to allow for better recognition of physical collaterals in view of their contribution to reducing credit risk (Schmit 2004).

Jimenez focused on limited set of determinants (collateral, type of lender and bank- borrower relationship), while controlling for the other explanatory variables such as the macroeconomic environment, characteristics of the borrower and of the loan (instrument, currency, maturity and size) and supported the viewpoint that collateral might decrease the screening efforts by banks for probable default but the same increases ex post probability of default of loan (Jimenez, 2004). Much of the literature available to research thoroughly discusses on banking sector, but there are many other financial institutions owned or operating (in the UK). Non-Banking financial institutions play a significant role in the economy (UK), reflected by the scale of their financial liabilities. While the potential knock-on effects of bank failures are reasonably clear, the wider disruption arising from the failure of non-banks is less obvious (Corder Mathew 2004). The statutory framework is helpful in recovering the non-performing assets, provided host of other things are put into place (Saha Kausick 2003). The Korean government adopted a policy of closing down financial institutions which were no longer viable because of an overhang of non-performing loans (NPLs), while inducing an early normalisation of those still viable through injection of public funds under the condition of their own intensive self-rescue efforts (Hyuang 2000).

Capital market financing in the form of public offer finance, loan on securities by the non-banking finance companies has resulted in too much exposure to over-heated stock markets. Therefore, the regulatory restrictions on capital market exposure are a welcome as it reduces the credit and operational risks (Crisil 2006). The risks faced by the finance companies emanates from fund-based activities rather than executive defaults (Crisil 2006)[6].

The risk continnum designed by the CRISIL for finance companies in India is represented below:

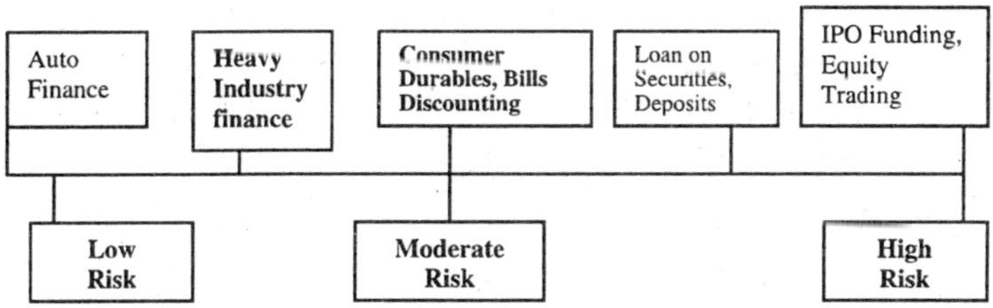

Source: Crisil Rating Scan (2006) – Rating methodology/Finance Sector

Figure 1: Risk Spectrum for Asset Financing Companies[7]

In order to diversify the operational risk, the finance companies witnessed a shift away from fixed deposits and bank funding to tradable securities like debentures and commercial papers. Finance companies with strong patronage from holding companies are issuing participatory notes. This has reduced the risks faced in fund raising to fund their long-term lending activities. Also, the lending profile witnessing shift from traditional leasing, and hire purchase financing, to remunerative education and health financing (CARE 2006). The Basel II recommendations on risk management for banking institutions have put severe constraints on lending and fund raising. However, they can mitigate the troubles faced by the industry (Saurina 2004). In a syndicated loan, two or more lenders come together to finance a loan to a borrower. Banks tend to decrease their credit risk by participating into syndicated loans. The division of a large loan into smaller homogenous parts leads to lower granularity and the borrower-specific risks get diversified in the process. Benefits of credit risk diversification are well understood and Basel II regulations recognize them explicitly. Non bank institutions in US are also more likely to participate in the riskier tranches of a multi-facility loan (Pankaj Kumar 2006). What explains the banks that don't manage their risks through the loan sales market? One possibility is that loans with private information are hard to sell at arm's length unless a bank has established a strong reputation over time in this market. In fact, the recent results by Dahiya, Puri, and Saunders are consistent with this view. The extant empirical literature for non-financial firms indicates that active risk management through both internal capital markets (e.g. scale and diversification) and through active engagement in the external capital markets (e.g. active use of derivatives) provide ways to manage liquidity and cash flow and achieve higher investment (Sinan Cebenoyan 2001).

CONCLUSION

The chapter began with comprehensive analysis of earnings and business profile, previous research works on macro economy and corporate earnings, categorization of non-banking finance companies, followed by the approaches to measure overall performance; financial ratio approach, shareholders' wealth in financial institutions, cost control strategies, and finally ended with risk management approaches.

NOTES

1. Reserve Bank of India has amended the classification of Non-Banking Finance Companies vide its circular issued by Department of NBS dated 6.12.2006.
2. Creating demand by making innovations in services and instruments.
3. Economic Value Added=Earnings before Interest and Taxes *(1-Tax rate)–(Operating Capital *Weighted Average Cost of Capital)
4. Networth is the net value that can be realized by the shareholders' value, if the company winds up the operation at once. It is interchangeably used as book value or networth.
5. Market Value Added is the difference between the market price of total stock and subscribed stock. It is given by the equation MVA = (Shares Outstanding * Stock Price)–Total common equity
6. see for further readings: CRISIL RatingScan Criteria/Finance Sector–Rating Methodology available *online: www.crisil.org.in*
7. *Source:* CRISIL RatingScan: Industry Comments–Criteria/ Finance Sector–Rating Methodology

3

PERFORMANCE MEASUREMENT OF FINANCIAL INSTITUTIONS–A STRATEGIC METHODOLOGY

INTRODUCTION

Almost in all the available literature on finance point out that the strategy of the management be it short-term or long-term is to maximize the wealth of the shareholders either by increasing the market value through perceived financial performance of the company or by increasing the realizable value of equity of shareholders ESW-NW (George Foster et al. 2002, Penman Stephen et al. 2001, Brigham et al. 2002, Raj Besant et al.1989, Ang et al & Peterson et al.1984). The objective of maximizing the value of equity, be it market value ESW-MV or additions to NW, is explored by accountants, academicians and the chief executives. Executive decisions on mergers and acquisitions is not only consolidate the position of a company, but also improve the performance (Chanda Rupa 2005). Mergers and acquisitions increase the value of the shareholders equity and consolidation of the financial statements of holding company boosts the shareholders' fund ESW-NW. A manager who perceives that he or she has the ability to increase the market value of a company attempts at, increasing the value of shareholders' funds ESW-NW by maximizing the returns allocation (George Foster 2002). Since objective of reserve allocation is to retain the earnings within the company, the strategy of the management increases the availability of internal funds, and also brings down the costs.

Openness to foreign competition puts pressure on domestic financial firms to improve their productivity, services and also gives them access to new technologies thereby improves the performance of the company (Kantawala et al 2004, Chanda Rupa et al 2005). It is important that in maximizing the equity value of a firm, managers should take steps to increase the cash flows both now and in the future and the earnings are keys to increasing the ESW-MV (Brigham 2002). A Bank's performance vis-à-vis its competitors' can be judged by using the shareholders wealth as performance measure and the measure is useful for taking decisions on consolidation of the banks, (Hyung-Gon Ro 2000). The previous work on increasing ESW focus mainly on the market value or the enterprise value EV[1] to access the value created by the performance

Hempel and Yawitz who have worked extensively on the maximization of the share value of the financial instituions, designed the foundation of the work on from the premise that "Wealth maximisation is the maximisation of the discounted cash benefits to shareholders" (Hempel and Yawitz 1977). Examiners will look at the composition of bank profits to determine whether they come from a solid operating base[2] or are driven by one-time gains, such as those generated by the sale of assets. Examiners regard earnings as the first line of defense against loan defaults and other unforeseen events. The maximization of share value is driven by the earnings coming from a solid operating base and is useful for the acquirer, (Whalen 1988). Various measures are used to measure performance of financial institutions' like competitor's earnings, market price of the share, net interest income, and branch profits. Since some of the financial institutions may be unlisted in the stock market, the data on market price could not be ascertained, in those situations the ESW-NW or shareholders' fund is useful to tackle the issue, (Raj Besant 1989). Sinkey (1977) proposed a second type of early-warning system that uses stock-market data to identify deteriorating condition. These models assume stock markets are efficient and that the underlying stochastic process governing stock returns is stable. Many distress prediction models use the Operating Profit[3], Current Ratio[4], and receivable among other variables to gauge the deterioration in the performance (Altman et. Al 1977, Lo 1984, and Gupta 1983).

Speed (1991) tested differences in performance between groups of companies on such variables as marketing practices, strategies, and organisational characteristics. Generally, the research on shareholders' wealth is based on ESW-MV. The measurement of shareholders' wealth using ESW-NW, i.e., shareholders' fund is useful when the unlisted companies are studied, and in the absence of active trading. The book value of equity measures depreciated past investment. Because the amount invested is likely to be highly correlated with the expected cash flows of the investment, one would expect the book value of equity and expected cash flow to be highly correlated, Berk Jonathan (1997). In fund-based activities of financial services company, the sources of finance is important as the procurement of funds at cheapest possible cost improves profitability, the performance, Kshirsagar (2003). Though, the profitability can be improved by reduction of cost, the volume of business is crucial to the performance measurement. Many of the research support this argument as far as financial services is concerned as the sustained business volume boost the confidence of the stakeholders (Khan 2003, Brigham 2002, Penman 2001).

One of the key performance measures for financial services industry in India, in the wake of prudential norms for provisioning, will be the scale of non-performing loans. Hence, controlling the non-performing loans will improve the overall performance (Saha Kausick 2003). Earnings are a key input to augment capital required for supporting growth and absorbing losses. Earnings also directly influence a company's ability to attract equity and debt. If the expectation of income is known and stationary (and it surely would become known), then investors' wealth ESW-NW is also stable inspite of variations in value. The use of financial ratios in evaluating a firm's performance has been vehemently opposed by many authors (George Foster 2002). The least, it can be used for comparison of intra-industry performance and it just gives the representative picture, not the actual position.

SHAREHOLDERS' WEALTH IN THE FINANCIAL SERVICES INDUSTRY

In the financial services industry in India, the valuation of shareholders' wealth based on market value is fraught with dangers of insider trading and also the stock exchanges are becoming integrated with the world markets. Moreover, it is difficult to value the equity shares, if the companies' shares are not actively traded and/or unlisted (Ingres 2006). Further, the problem gets accentuated with only a few players dominant in the asset finance industry, whose shares are listed and actively traded. As far as Tamil Nadu is concerned, there are many small companies are operating in asset financing and many of which are not deposit taking finance companies. Further, they are family businesses of local wealthy group. Hence, the use of ESW based on networth is an appropriate measure for performance evaluation[5]. Abatement of rise in bad loans will improve the efficiency of the finance companies and increase the profitability, the returns to scale. Economies of scale is affected by size, operational area and competition (Mohanty Jaya 2003). The modaraba companies, non-banking finance companies, in Pakistan are providing finance directly to the industry and are able to establish a direct link between finance and industry unlike Islamic banks (Khan Tariquallah 1996).

The earnings of the asset finance companies operating in financial services industry come from core or fund-based business, non-core or fee-based business activities. The finance income from equipment leasing and interest income from hire purchase financing are the core operations. But the recent trend in earnings has been towards increasing non-core fee-based earnings such as insurance, bill discounting, travel and software development (Ingres 2006). The core expenses are incurred for operations. Finance charges, interest, administrative expenses, salary expenses, the operating expenses, are on the rise with the mobilization of public deposits have been severely restricted (Nisture Rupa 2001). Diversification into new business ventures such as credit cards, insurance, asset management either through separate division or subsidiaries (Seema Sagar 1999). The tightening of regulatory and supervisory framework for NBFCs has also been coterminous with the rapid product development and diversification, sweeping changes in technology along with trends indicating consolidation in the financial sector[6]. The earnings are affected by norms relating to income recognition and *provisioning* for non-performing assets (Taxmann 2004). Staffing expenses increases with the increase in competitors' wage as structure and inflation (Ritter Jay 2003). Kantawala (2004) has found there is a strong link between the utilization of operating assets and performance through financial ratios. The performance of the financial institutions can be measured in terms of increase in shareholders' wealth.

OPERATING ENVIRONMENT OF ASSET FINANCE COMPANIES

The product mix of Asset Finance Companies consists mainly of finance leases and hire purchase. These asset-based financing plans are designed in such a way that the cost of the asset with a reasonable rate of return is paid back during the tenor of the lease by the lessee. Hence, this type of financing is the major contributor to the credit risk of the Asset Finance Companies. The business of the asset finance companies contains both interest rate sensitive assets (Leased, Stock on Hire assets) and interest rate sensitive liabilities (bank loans, term loans, public deposits, and commercial papers, intercorporate deposits etc). Hence, the asset finance companies are facing interest rate risk. The uncertainties in cash flows from assets and outflow to liabilities expose these companies to liquidity risk. They are exposed to market risk through the uncertainties in returns from the investments in securities, subsidiaries and mutual funds. The asset finance companies are exposed to many threats, opportunities to grow dynamic and vibrant. The competitive environment threatening the asset finance companies is shown in Figure 1.

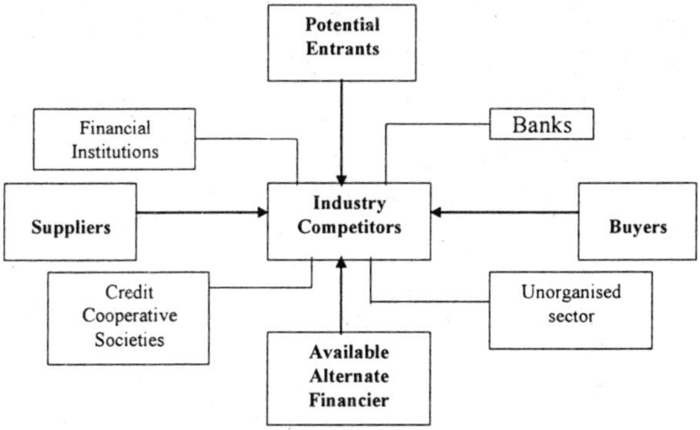

Figure 1 : Environmental Factors Driving Competition

The entry threats are driven by economies of scale such as resource mobilization and geographical spread of operations with different lines of business. Further, the reputed finance companies can mobilize huge resources with less effort at low cost due to brand equity of them. The capital requirements act as an effective barrier to entry. Though, capital requirement is only a meager sum but in effect, the requirement goes up on start of the business due to accessibility of public deposits and bank borrowings. The credit rating on borrowings programme denies funds to virtually new entrants. The stiff competition among the existing players and the mature equipment leasing, hire purchase market acts as an additional barrier. The competition comes from banks, financial institutions like insurance companies, public sector finance corporations. Exit barriers like repayment of public deposits, realization of non-performing assets to meet other liabilities act as effective barrier to go out of the business. The personal loans, collateral loans offered by the banks, financial institutions are the key substitutes or alternate financing sources. The credit worthiness of the high quality borrowers gives them edge to borrow funds at easier terms and low cost than an ordinary borrower. As suppliers of term loans, banks and financial institutions favour large-sized finance companies. The cost of borrowing will be high to newly established finance companies than an existing one. Therefore, the suppliers of funds have a bargaining power.

From the above literature, the author has identified the *Earnings, ESWealth-MV, IntCost* (interest cost), asset valuation as drivers of performance and other key dimensions of the performance through efficiency measurements are empirically tested on internal & industry aspects. The author has identified that there exist a gap in the research relating to measurement of cost, income and earnings dimensions. Besides, the previous research in measuring performance in terms of *ESWealth-MV* will be misleading *vis-à-vis* financial institutions, as many of them are not listed and/or actively traded to get the market quotes. The Shareholders' wealth based on market value has been given over-emphasis for measuring the performance by ignoring the fact that markets are prone to external shocks such as foreign direct investment, exchange rate, and finally, world economy. Though, many of the asset finance companies are not directly subjected to the external shocks listed above, the performance measurement based on net worth would be valid and reliable. The little attention has been paid to the operational costs and income aspects of the asset financing activities. Wide research has been carried out in the banking industry, which may be useful. But given the diverse activities of the banking, the results could be unreasonable and misleading if applied, as far as the asset finance companies are concerned.

RATIONALE BEHIND USING INCOME AS THE MEDIATING VARIABLE IN THE NETWORTH OF EQUITY SHARES (SHAREHOLDERS' FUNDS) IN NON-BANKING FINANCE SECTOR

There is a dearth of integrated bank performance analyses that use an interdisciplinary and multivariate perspective. Bank performance analysis has been implemented commonly through budgeting, measuring total deposits, and branch profits; the latter two measures generate retrospective information which cannot be used to gauge the potential of a bank to generate retail banking business. Budgeting is criticised for placing too much emphasis on items that are outside the management's sphere of influence, and focusing on expense items rather than overall earnings (Smith III and Schweikart 1992).

In its widest sense, a firm's performance objective can be interpreted as maximising the value of its shareholders' investments at sustainable levels; thus, in the long term, the critical measure of overall bank performance should be business earnings (Gup, Fraser, and Kolari 1989). Hence, the concept of wealth maximisation is reviewed first. Hempel and Yawitz who have addressed the principle of equity value maximisation in the context of financial institutions, start off from the premise that "Wealth maximisation is the maximisation of the discounted cash benefits (earnings) to shareholders" (Hempel and Yawitz 1977). They, then, proceed to identify the key variables in cash benefits as gross receipts from assets, cost of liabilities, overhead costs, taxes, earnings are expected to be examined for the different ways they may interact with these key variables.

With measurement of overall performance in mind, they produce four categories of key variables influencing the equity value, namely, spread management, control of overhead, liquidity management, capital management, and net interest income, NII. These categories are explained in the works of Hempel and Yawitz (1977) and De Lucia et al. (1987). It involves lot of efforts to control the overhead costs or non-interest expenses, which deals with the ability of the bank to hold down such expenses even while maintaining a reasonable spread. It is not always true that control of overhead costs if business mix decisions for increasing the net interest income[7] are not closely scrutinised for their impact on earnings.

The constraint of containing the overhead costs is in the context of non-interest income (that is, fee income), constraint is defined as the net non-interest income (that is, difference between non-interest income and non-interest expenses). The accounting method decisions interact with other key firms decisions such as mix of business, financing, and operating decisions. The diversity in the accounting in the treatment of depreciation, deferred taxes, and provisioning may result in distortion of profitability than less diverse income recognition standards (Foster George 2002). The treatment of expenses such as research and development, pension, and many others seriously affect the comparability of the financial statements of the same company (Dawson 1975). From 1997, the companies are required to report the comprehensive income plus net income to reflect fairness in income recognition. Comprehensive income includes net income plus several comprehensive income items[8] in the income statement (Brigham Eugene 2004) & (RBI 1998). Hence, the income (mainly, the business income) is used as mediating variable in this study.

APPROACH TO DATA ANALYSIS

In order to adopt strategic performance measurement tool, the book employs pooled or combined data approach. Methodology described as pooled "is one in which data are elements of both time series and cross section data" (Gujarati Damodar 2004). A time series is a set of observations on the values that a variable takes at different times. Such data may be collected at regular time intervals, like annually. Cross-sectional data "is one used to collect data on all variables at one point of time" (O'Sullivan & Rassel 1999). This approach is adopted in most econometric data collection. This approach is most useful for studies designed to collect information on trends or behaviour of variables over a period of time. In order to compare the events influenced the behaviour of one variable over a time horizon with another, the time series approach will be inadequate to make inferences. Alternatively, the cross sectional approach will be useless to test the variable movement when studying an important event, if it is not ex ante and ex post. Hence, pooled data collection to assess the impact of regulation on performance of asset finance companies over the time horizon viz., 1994-95 to 2003-04. The approach to macroeconomic variables is time series.

The work is designed in such a way that it is based on financial data, which are published. The secondary data is considered as the most appropriate to the measure the dimensional effects of the performance of the asset finance companies in Tamil Nadu in this study. The secondary data is the most appropriate research design as it can enable the author to identify the divergence in practice and collect information on financial variables over a time horizon. The information obtained from the asset finance companies can then be generalized to an entire population (Kerlinger & Lee 2000). The secondary data is practically, a quantitative method that requires standardized information in order to define or describe variables or to study the relationships between the variables. The current study is secondary data oriented and relies on the industrial publications. The research is designed to bring out the casual relationship within various dimensions of the performance and business earnings (*Income*) as the mediating factor and the outcome of performance in maximizing the shareholders' wealth.

FINANCIAL VARIABLES AND DATA COLLECTION

Data were collected by means of collection of annual reports which are secondary data in the form of published documents from various sources viz., companies' published annual reports, statutory returns filed with Registrar of Companies, publications of associations and rating agencies from 1994-95 to 2003-03. The publications of Reserve Bank of India on the performance of Non-Banking Financial Companies are used as industrial data. Inspections were conducted in the offices of Registrar of Companies situated in Chennai & Coimbatore to collect data on the privately held asset finance companies. The investment finance companies, loan finance companies, housing finance companies, and miscellaneous non-banking finance companies were excluded from the scope of study. Only the asset finance companies, whose business mix is not less than 60% in asset financing i.e., equipment leasing and hire purchase (as per reclassification of NBFCs by the Reserve Bank in 2006[9]) financing. Personal visits were undertaken to the companies to have first hand knowledge on the operations and the divergence in data. The geographical area under study is confined to Tamil Nadu. Further, the asset finance companies, which are registered and reporting to the Reserve Bank of India, Chennai is alone included in the sample. Personal discussions were conducted with the executives of the companies in the sample. Assurance was given to the respondent company that the data collected will be kept in confidence and will be used only for academic research purposes after analysis. Of more than 150 finance companies operating in the state, only 43 asset finance companies are registered and reporting to Reserve Bank as on 31.3.2006. The deposit position of the reporting asset finance companies as on 31.3.2006 is shown in the Appendix A.

Initially, the deposit position of the asset finance companies as at the end of 31st March 2004 is taken to identify the potential sample. In order to study the current scenario and to drop the companies that have wound up their operations during 2004-05, the crucial date for identifying the sample has been revised to 31st March 2006. Asset finance companies with public deposits of less than Rs.100 lakhs and the public sector asset finance companies were dropped from the purview of the study. The idea behind dropping the asset finance companies with deposits less Rs.100 lakhs is that they commenced their operations only after 1999. The public sector asset finance companies were kept out of the study because their operational strategies are formulated and closely monitored by the state government. They have little functional and managerial freedom unlike the ones in private sector. The sampling procedure used in the book was stratified random sampling. The stratification has been based on the quantum of public deposits held by them as on 31st March 2006. Table 1 gives a view of the companies based on the stratification (Secondary data used in SPSS 15.0).

Table 1
Deposit Position and Nature of Management of the Stratification

Strata	*No*	*Private*	*Public Sector*	*Total Deposits (In Lakhs)*
Asset Finance Companies >= 10000 Lakhs	4	2	2	150,093.00
AFCs with deposits <10000,=>1000 Lakhs	10	9	1	38,721.00
AFCs with deposits <1000, =>500 Lakhs	4	4	0	2,437.00
AFCs with deposits <500, =>100 Lakhs	8	8	0	1,813.00
AFCs with deposits >100 Lakhs	17	17	0	656.00

Based on the stratification done as above, the sample has been identified within it and prior studies were compared to make the sample as far as possible true representative of the population (43 Asset Finance Companies). Table 2 gives the companies drawn into the sample based on the stratification and after adopting elimination criteria.

Table 2
Characteristics of the Sample Based on Stratification

Name of the Company	*Location*	*No of Branches in Tamil Nadu (31.3.2004)*	*Deposit Held (Rs. in Lakhs)*
Sundaram Finance Ltd.	Chennai	127	73,112
First Leasing Company of India Ltd.	Chennai	16	8,641
India Cements Capital & Finance Ltd.	Chennai	16	1,565
Newlink Overseas Finance Ltd.	Chennai	10	1,257
Carthic Credits Ltd.	Coimbatore	3	267
L.R.N. Finance Ltd.	Salem	3	117

Source: Annual Reports & Statutory Returns filed with Registrar of Companies.

The financial statements of the companies were examined in detail for accounting diversity. The accounting diversity found in the course of examination, was eliminated through recasting of the financial statements so that comparability and reliability of the data is ensured. The merger and acquisition, public issue, and all other relevant impacting events were taken into account for data analysis. The change in accounting year affects the financial statements. Hence, the author has taken efforts to eliminate the impact by computing the figures with the available data and after discussions with companies' executives.

DATA ANALYSIS–A METHODOLOGICAL APPROACH

The data collected were analyzed for the entire sample. Data analyses were performed with Statistical Package for Social Sciences *(SPSS)* using techniques that included descriptive statistics, correlation analysis and *AMOS* Package for Structural Equation Modeling and Bayesian Estimation and testing.

STRUCTURAL EQUATION MODELLING-AN INNOVATIVE APPROACH

The main study used structural equation modeling *(SEM)* because of two advantages: "(1) estimation of multiple and interrelated dependence relationships, and (2) the ability to represent unobserved concepts in these relationships and account for measurement error in the estimation process" (Hair et al.,1998, p.584). In other words, a series of split but independent multiple regressions were simultaneously estimated by *SEM*. Therefore, the direct and indirect effects were identified (Tate, 1998). However, a series of separate multiple regressions had to be established based on "theory, a priori experience, and the research objectives to distinguish which independent variables predict each dependent variable" (Hair et al, 1998, p.584). In addition, because *SEM* considers a measurement error, the reliability of the predictor variable was improved. Structural Equation Modeling was conducted with *AMOS 16.0* (an upgraded version of *AMOS 7.0*). *AMOS 7.0* (Arbuckle and Wothke, 2006), a computer program for formulating, fitting and testing structural equation models to observed data was used for *SEM* and the data preparation was conducted with *SPSS 15.0*.

Linear structural equation models *(SEMs)* are widely used in sociology, econometrics, management, biology, and other sciences. A *SEM* (without free parameters has two parts: a probability distribution (in the Normal case specified by a set of linear structural equations and a covariance matrix among the "error" or "disturbance" terms), and an associated path diagram corresponding to the casual relations among variables specified by the structural equations and the correlations among the error terms. It is often thought that the path diagram is nothing more than a heuristic device for illustrating the assumptions of the model. However, in this work, the author will show how path diagrams can be used to solve a number of complex problems in structural equation modeling.

Structural equation models with latent variables *(SEM)* are more and more often used to analyze relationships among variables in marketing and consumer research (refer Bollen 1989, Schumacker & Lomax 1996, or Batisa-Foguet & Coenders 2000, for an introduction and Bagozzi 1994 for applications to marketing research). Some reasons for the widespread use of these models are their parsimony (they belong to the family of linear models), their ability to model complex systems (where simultaneous and reciprocal relationships may be present, such as relationship between profitability and economic growth), and their ability to model relationships among non-observable variables (such as the external shocks in the *SEM-ESW* model) while taking measurement errors into account (which are usually sizeable in small sample and can result in biased estimates if ignored). As is usually recommended, a confirmatory factor analysis *(CFA)* model is first specified to account for the measurement of relationships from latent to observable variables. In our case, the latent variables are the earnings, business, cost, and equity shareholders' wealth-with and without deflator dimensions and the observed variables are: the interest income, dividend income, lease rent, and hire purchase finance charges for the earnings dimensions; non-business income, business expenses, and non-business expenses for the business dimension; loan interest, finance charges, provision for non-performing assets, staff compensation (salary and other benefits) for cost control dimension; earnings, expenses, profitability for equity shareholders' wealth (performance) dimension. The relationships among latent variables cannot be tested until a well-fitting *CFA* model has been reached. In our case, the relationships among overall performance of asset finance companies, the mediating influence of profit and income (with deflator) with the cost, business, and earnings dimensions are quite interesting from the academic research standpoint. This modeling sequence stresses the importance of the goodness of fit assessment. As a combination of regression, path and factor analyses, in *SEM*, each predictor is used with its associated uncontrolled error and; unlike regression analyses, predictor multi-collinearity does not affect the model results.

EVALUATION OF MODEL FIT AND VARIOUS MEASURES OF FITNESS

According to the usual procedures, checking the statistical and substantive validity of estimates, the convergence of the estimation procedure, the empirical identification of the model, the statistical significance of the parameters, and the goodness of fit to the covariance matrix assess the goodness of fit. Since complex models are inevitably mis-specified to a certain extent, the standard x^2 test of the hypothesis of perfect fit to the population covariance matrix is given less importance than measures of the degree of approximation between the model and the population covariance matrix. The roots mean squared error of approximation *(RMSEA)* is selected as such a measure. Values equal to 0.05 or lower are generally considered to be acceptable (Brown &Cudeck 1993). The sampling distribution for the *RMSEA* can be derived, which makes it possible to compute confidence intervals.

These intervals allow authors to test for close fit and not only for exact fit, as the χ^2 statistic does. If both extremes of the confidence interval are below 0.05, then the hypothesis of close fit is rejected in favor of the hypothesis of better than close fit. If both extremes of he confidence interval are above 0.05, then the hypothesis of close is rejected in favor of the hypothesis of bad fit.

Several well-known goodness of fit indices were used to evaluate model fit: the chi-square x^2, the comparative fit index *(CFI)*, the unadjusted goodness-of-fit indices *(GFI)*, the normal fit index *(NFI)*, the Tucker- Lewis Index *(TLI)*, the root mean square error of approximation *(RMSEA)* and the standardized root mean square error residual *(SRMR)*.

BAYESIAN ESTIMATION OF NORMAL DISTRIBUTION AND TESTING IN SEM

With modern computers and software, a Bayesian approach to structural equation modeling *(SEM)* is now possible. Posterior distributions over the parameters of a structural equation model can be approximated to arbitrary precision with *AMOS*, even for small samples. Being able to compute the posterior over the parameters allows us to address several issues of academic and practical issues. First, prior knowledge about the parameters may be incorporated into the modeling process in *AMOS*. Second, we need not rely on asymptotic theory when the sample size is too small, a practice which has been shown to be misleading for inference and goodness-of-fit tests in *SEM* (Boomsma 1983). Third, the class of models that can be handled is no longer restricted to just-identified or over-identified models. Finally, the *SEM* estimates the cause-effect between the variables. Whereas each identifying assumption must be taken as given in the classical approach, in a Bayesian approach some of these assumptions can be specified with perhaps more realistic uncertainty.

HYPOTHESIS DEVELOPMENT TO MEASURE PERFORMANCE

Mediation refers to a process or mechanism through which one variable (i.e., exogenous) causes variation in another variable (i.e., endogenous). Studies designed to test for moderation may provide stronger tests for mediation than the partial and whole covariance approaches typically used (e.g., Baron & Kenny 1986; Bing, Davison, LeBreton, & LeBreton 2002, James & Bren 1984). It is useful to distinguish between moderation and mediation. Moderation carries with it no connotation of causality, unlike mediation, which implies causal order. Based on the arguments discussed in the previous chapters and this chapter the author formulated the following hypotheses for dimensions of performance of asset finance companies in succeeding sections.

- The dimensions of cost influence the profit as the mediating factor.
- The dimensions of income influence the profit as the mediating factor.
- The dimensions of cost positively influence the shareholders' wealth

The mediator hypothesis is supported if the interaction path (*Cost, Income,* X Profit) are significant. There may also be significant main effects for the predictors (Cost, Income) and mediator (Profit). Therefore, the author searches the existence of relationship between cost, income are fully or partially mediated by Profit. The hypothesized mediated models are given in the Figures 2-6.

ANALYSIS OF SOURCES OF FUNDS AND ITS USES IN ASSET FINANCE COMPANIES

Table 3
Position of Net Owned Funds of the Asset Finance Companies in Tamil Nadu

	Net Owned Funds (Amount Rupees in Lakhs)					
	Sub Sample					
Sample Data/Year	*Strata I*	*Strata II*	*Strata III*	*Strata IV*	*Sample Total*	*Industrial Average*
2 Years MVA	19027	7018	318	96	26460	162430
3 Years MVA	22059	7581	364	100	30104	191856
4 Years MVA	24954	7546	393	105	32998	240827
5 Years MVA	27099	8187	421	108	35815	248877
6 Years MVA	28765	8730	441	109	38045	251655
7 Years MVA	29715	9178	457	117	39468	253958
8 Years MVA	29526	9531	477	123	39656	242243
9 Years MVA	29552	9967	485	131	40135	234569
10 Years MVA	29963	10407	494	145	41008	231885
Average	29963	10407	494	145	41008	231885
CAGR	7.44	9.59	8.88	12.20	8.07	2.20

Source: Published annual reports of the companies, *Industrial Average*-Performance study of NBFCs by Reserve Bank, *MVA*-Moving Average *CAGR*-Compounded Annual Growth Rate

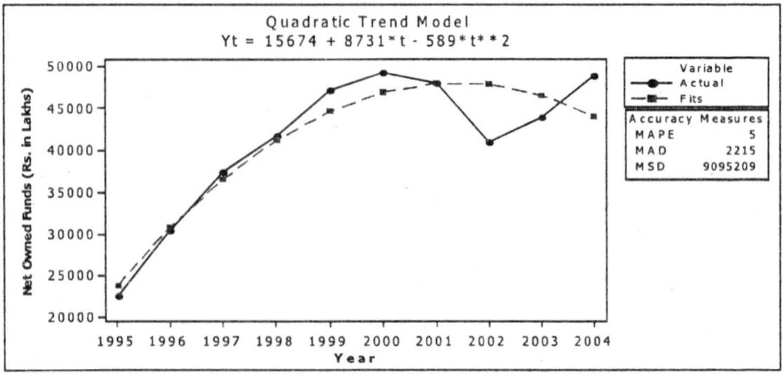

Figure 2 : Plot mapping Trends in Net Owned Funds of Asset Finance Companies

Table 3 and Plot in figure 2 reveal the trends in the net owned funds of the asset finance companies. Prior to the enforcement of new regulations i.e., effective from 1999-2000, the net owned funds of the asset finance companies is in fairly stable growth trend. According to Rakesh Mohan (2004), the linking of net owned funds (NOF), capital adequacy, and rating requirements are aimed at protecting the interests of the depositors. The companies promoted by big industrial groups are enjoying substantial free reserves in the form of share premium due to new issues in 1994-95 to 95-96. Taking advantage of the booming capital market, the companies come up with book-building issues to boost their capital position. With the enforcement of regulations linking mobilization of public deposits to net owned funds, all the asset finance companies have been compelled to increase the net owned funds. The improvement in net owned funds during 1998-2000 is mainly due to substantial issue of the new shares and preferential shares. It attribute the reasons for decline in the trend are due to stock market scams affecting new issues, frequent closure of finance companies and increasing cost of public deposits due to competition from financial institutions and banks. However, the compounded annual growth is more than 8% and even surpassed the national industrial trend.

Table 4 and times series plot figure 3 reveal the trends in the shareholders' net worth or funds. During the initial phase, i.e., from 1995-2001, the shareholders' fund is in increasing at a fairly steady growth. They attribute the reasons for this trend are due to substantial retention of earnings, and enhanced allocation of earnings to internal reserves. The hire-purchase finance companies in the non-bank finance sector are able to cover their interest charges due to high return on net worth, earnings in this activity has considerably risen thanks to booming economy and consumers' favorable disposition in acquiring movable assets (Kantawala 2004). Again, the reason for steadiness in growth is due to floating new issues by the new entrants to their group companies and promoters. The skewness in trend during 2000-2003 is because of increase in cost of operations, which affected the profitability profile of

Table 4
Position of Shareholders' Funds of Asset Finance Companies

	Shareholders' Funds (Amount Rupees in Lakhs)					
	Sub Sample					
Sample Data/Year	*Strata I*	*Strata II*	*Strata III*	*Strata IV*	*Sample Total*	*Industrial Average*
2 Years MVA	20005	7368	329	107	27809	183081
3 Years MVA	22840	8147	372	113	31472	217345
4 Years MVA	25809	8794	400	117	35121	269009
5 Years MVA	28512	9456	426	119	38514	272661
6 Years MVA	30910	10077	449	122	41558	274638
7 Years MVA	33656	10578	469	130	44833	276509
8 Years MVA	34895	11150	487	136	46667	264505
9 Years MVA	36424	11794	496	144	48858	256977
10 Years MVA	38014	12511	507	158	51190	254853
Average	38014	12511	507	158	51190	254853
CAGR	11.78	12.21	8.93	11.61	11.86	2.59

Source: Published annual reports of the companies, *Industrial Average*-Performance study of NBFCs by Reserve Bank, *MVA*-Moving Average *CAGR*-Compounded Annual Growth Rate

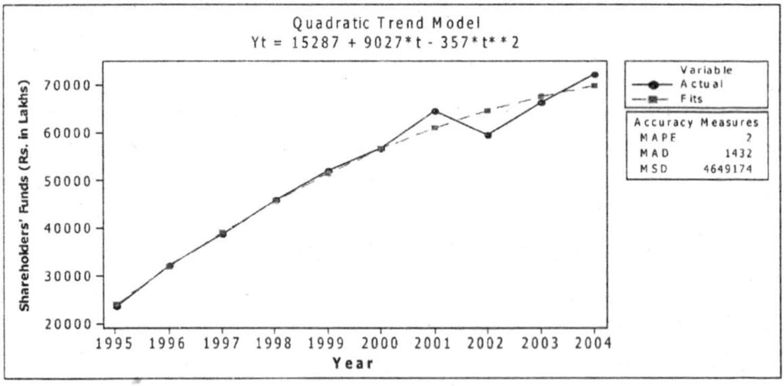

Figure 3 : Plot mapping Trends in Shareholders' Funds of Asset Finance Companies

the companies, particularly those operating in traditional areas of business like leasing and hire purchase activities. The financing cost can be brought down, if the banks and financial institutions raise the internal accruals through more retention of earnings. It is the cheapest source of finance, not costless given the opportunity cost (George Foster 2002). But the asset finance companies in Tamil Nadu are having a formidable compounded annual growth when compared with industry performance.

Table 5

Position of Generation of Internal Funds of Asset Finance Companies

Internal Funds (Amount Rupees in Lakhs)						
	Sub Sample					
Sample Data/Year	*Strata I*	*Strata II*	*Strata III*	*Strata IV*	*Sample Total*	*Industrial Average*
2 Years MVA	9238	3680	132	14	13063	68443
3 Years MVA	10508	4205	88	11	14812	94896
4 Years MVA	11208	4365	82	12	15667	59104
5 Years MVA	12135	4293	80	9	16518	51353
6 Years MVA	10206	3900	48	4	14158	31698
7 Years MVA	8858	3697	45	4	12605	16051
8 Years MVA	7907	3513	32	5	11456	8733
9 Years MVA	7183	3124	38	4	10349	11665
10 Years MVA	7381	2811	47	5	10592	15864
Average	7381	2811	47	5	10592	15864
CAGR	0.00	-53.68	0.00	-0.56	0.00	0.00

Source: Published annual reports of the companies, *Industrial Average*-Performance study of NBFCs by Reserve Bank, *MVA*-Moving Average *CAGR*-Compounded Annual Growth Rate.

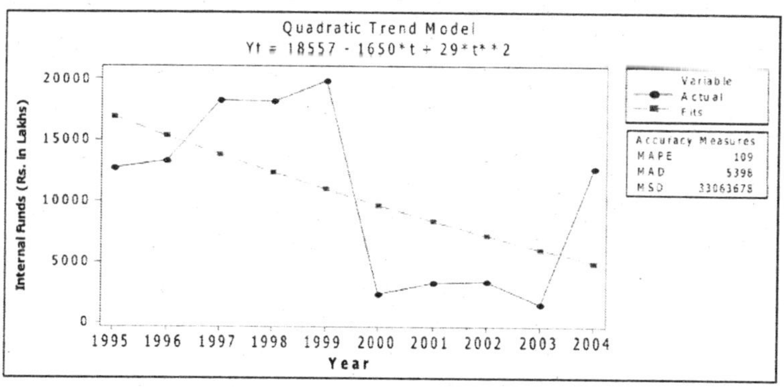

Figure 4 : Plot Mapping Trends in Internal Funds of Asset Finance Companies

Table 5 and Times Series plot figure 4 reveal the skewed distribution in the internal funds generation by the asset finance companies. The positive skewness during 1996-1999 is attributed to higher retention of earnings, inclination of management to mobilize long-term internal funds in the form of equity and preferential capital. The sharp downward trend in 2000 is attributed to high utilization of internal earnings to retire the debenture capital and repayment of deposits in the wake of closure of many finance companies due to raising non-performing assets, asset stripping. The enforcement of regulations on group exposure and capital market exposure norms, and shift to new tax regime have affected the internal funds position of the asset finance companies. However, the positive upward movement during 2003-04 is due to moderation in tax liability provided scope of higher retention of earnings.

Table 6
Position of External Funds Mobilized by Asset Finance Companies

	External Funds (Amount Rupees in Lakhs)					
	Sub Sample					
Sample Data/Year	*Strata I*	*Strata II*	*Strata III*	*Strata IV*	*Sample Total*	*Industrial Average*
2 Years MVA	4583	418	167	83	5251	97717
3 Years MVA	6159	690	231	52	7132	55806
4 Years MVA	7881	1152	249	60	9342	48204
5 Years MVA	8966	1185	155	-13	10293	-23158
6 Years MVA	10112	1465	74	-40	11612	-76484
7 Years MVA	8748	47	55	-52	8799	-107101
8 Years MVA	7558	-263	20	-56	7259	-84903
9 Years MVA	6858	-745	27	-63	6076	-118131
10 Years MVA	6311	-670	3	-56	5589	-127755
Average	6311	-670	3	-56	5589	-127755
CAGR	-17.19	-35.16	0.00	-25.42	-19.51	0.00

Source: Published annual reports of the companies, *Industrial Average*-Performance study of NBFCs by Reserve Bank, *MVA*-Moving Average *CAGR*-Compounded Annual Growth Rate.

Table 6 and Times Series Plot in Figure 5 reveal the asymmetric distribution in external funds. In the initial phase,

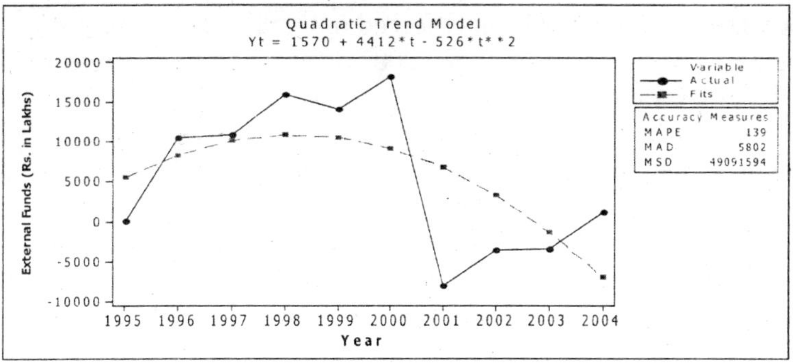

Figure 5 : Plot mapping Trends in External Funds of Asset Finance Companies

i.e., 1995-2000, the bank lending to finance companies is unrestricted. With the issue of guidelines and restrictions on exposure to non-banking finance set by the banks, the term loan disbursements by the banks to finance companies have fallen more significantly in 2001. But there is an identification issue: observed changes in corporate bank and non-bank finance will reflect movements in both the supply of and demand for external funds and it is difficult to disentangle the two (Ursel Baumann 2005). Further the closure of many finance companies and rampancy of mismanagement have forced the banks to desist from active lending except to high profile finance companies. Finance companies with strong patronage from holding companies are issuing participatory notes. This has reduced the risks faced in fund raising to fund their long-term lending activities (CARE 2006). However, the upward movement in the trend in 2002-2004 is due to inability of the finance companies to access the capital market, which witnessed integration with global markets. With the relaxation of foreign investment in financial sector, the cost of financing is coming down and the avenues to raise the funds are increasing (Stulz 1999). The negative CAGR has been vindicated by the above conditions.

Table 7 and Time Series plot 6 reveal the positively skewed distribution. They attribute that the regulations on access to public deposits, exposure to subsidiaries by the big finance companies have not been enforced in totality and vigorously as they have been during 2000-2003. More convincing reason is that the finance companies have no longer, access to debenture capital issues, due to raising cost of debenture issues and rating requirements. However, the recent relaxation of norms on issue of commercial paper is helping the asset finance companies to have access to unsecured funds. The compounded annual growth reveals that the asset finance companies in the state have more access to these funds than the national players.

Table 7
Position of Unsecured Funds of Asset Finance Companies

	Unsecured Funds (Amount Rupees in Lakhs)					
	Sub Sample					
Sample Data/Year	*Strata I*	*Strata II*	*Strata III*	*Strata IV*	*Sample Total*	*Industrial Average*
2 Years MVA	51792	14549	753	266	67361	218104
3 Years MVA	60234	16759	973	312	78278	295130
4 Years MVA	64633	18300	1087	361	84381	360865
5 Years MVA	71255	18729	1172	356	91512	382931
6 Years MVA	73554	18628	1178	334	93694	379060
7 Years MVA	75436	18684	1210	313	95643	372009
8 Years MVA	77174	18524	1235	300	97234	362724
9 Years MVA	78065	18174	1262	296	97798	347350
10 Years MVA	79867	17744	1286	300	99197	338582
Average	79867	17744	1286	300	99197	338582
CAGR	8.14	0.20	12.15	5.41	6.75	3.77

Source: Published annual reports of the companies, *Industrial Average*-Performance study of NBFCs by Reserve Bank, *MVA*-Moving Average *CAGR*-Compounded Annual Growth Rate

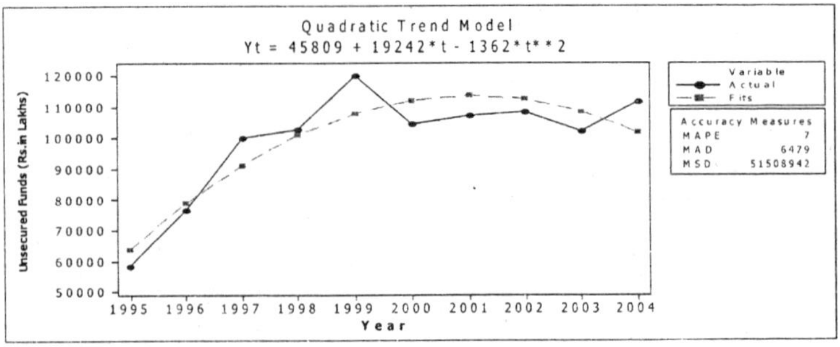

Figure 6 : Plot mapping Trends in Unsecured Funds of Asset Finance Companies

Table 8
Position of Secured Funds of Asset Finance Companies

	Secured Funds (Amount Rupees in Lakhs)					
	Sub Sample					
Sample Data/Year	*Strata I*	*Strata II*	*Strata III*	*Strata IV*	*Sample Total*	*Industrial Average*
2 Years MVA	51448	13172	149	48	64817	182908
3 Years MVA	54265	13167	99	49	67581	232226
4 Years MVA	56636	14051	106	58	70851	269145
5 Years MVA	52025	16415	104	57	68602	286795
6 Years MVA	53629	19657	117	62	73465	312488
7 Years MVA	57711	22688	117	69	80585	331579
8 Years MVA	61698	25357	120	76	87250	382160
9 Years MVA	69590	26991	127	76	96784	422973
10 Years MVA	78873	28730	139	75	107818	461356
Average	78873	28730	139	75	107818	461356
CAGR	12.80	13.20	-0.86	9.94	12.85	20.03

Source: Published annual reports of the companies, *Industrial Average*-Performance study of NBFCs by Reserve Bank, *MVA*-Moving Average *CAGR*-Compounded Annual Growth Rate.

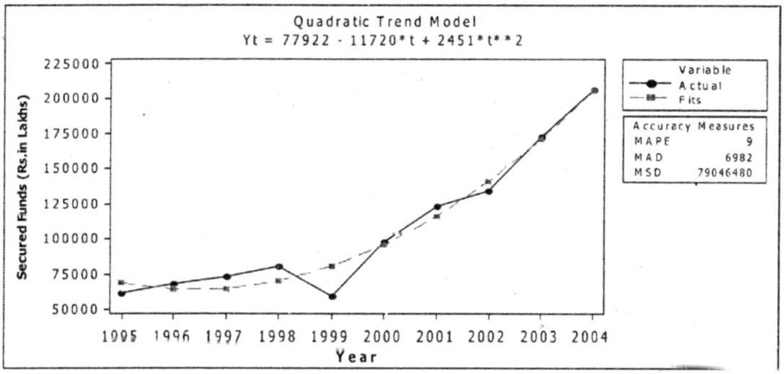

Figure 7 : Plot mapping Trends in Secured Funds of Asset Finance Companies

Table 8 and Time Series Plot 7 reveal the symmetrical distribution. It attribute that the asset finance companies in the state, have fairly easy access to the secured funds except in 1999. The stability of secured funds in the form of non-convertible debenture, banks' working capital assistance, and cash credit accommodation is attributed to restrictions on access to public deposits, high cost of funds for unsecured loans, and availability of collateralized assets for availing cash credits. Moreover, the covenants are more flexible to secured loans than the unsecured loans. Hence, the dependence on secured funds is at steadying growth. This is vindicated by the higher rate of compounded annual growth.

Table 9
Position of Capital Adequacy of Asset Finance Companies

	Capital to Risk Adjusted Assets					
	Sub Sample					
Sample Data/Year	*Strata I*	*Strata II*	*Strata III*	*Strata IV*	*Sample Average*	*Industrial Average*
2 Years MVA	16	24	34	11	21	N.A
3 Years MVA	16	23	32	11	21	N.A
4 Years MVA	17	23	29	14	21	N.A
5 Years MVA	18	22	28	16	21	N.A
6 Years MVA	18	21	27	19	21	N.A
7 Years MVA	19	21	27	21	22	N.A
8 Years MVA	19	20	27	22	22	N.A
9 Years MVA	19	20	26	24	22	N.A
10 Years MVA	18	21	26	26	23	N.A
Average	18	21	26	26	23	N.A
CAGR	0.38	-0.26	-3.81	15.08	2.31	N.A

Source: Published annual reports of the companies, *Industrial Average*-Performance study of NBFCs by Reserve Bank, *MVA*-Moving Average *CAGR*-Compounded Annual Growth Rate *N.A*-not available

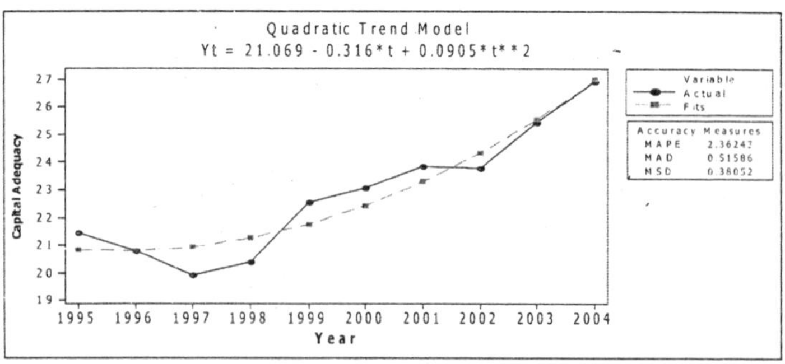

Figure 8 : Plot mapping Trends in Capital Adequacy of Asset Finance Companies

Table 9 and Times Series Plot 8 bring to light the positively skewed distribution except 1997-98. They attribute the reasons for increasing positive trend is due to linking of capital adequacy for resource mobilization, viz., bank borrowings, public deposits, and riskiness of assets. Schmit presented the first empirical results on the default and loss severity of leases by implementing a non-parametric simulation based on ex ante and ex post data on four types of leases. He felt that there is an urgent need to review the capital adequacy proposals in order to allow for better recognition of physical collaterals in view of their contribution to reducing credit risk (Schmit 2004). In 1997 & 1998, many of the automobile manufacturers witnessed contraction of sales and economy was also on downward trend, which led to low off take and the poor credit recovery due to asset stripping. However, the economy is on positive track since 1999 and riskiness of assets was diversified through higher volume in hire purchase activities than in leasing. The linking of capital adequacy to resource mobilization forces the asset finance companies to diversify their asset profile and minimize the risk.

Table 10
Position of Investments of Asset Finance Companies

	Investments (Amount Rupees in Lakhs)					
	Sub Sample					
Sample Data/Year	*Strata I*	*Strata II*	*Strata III*	*Strata IV*	*Sample Total*	*Industrial Average*
2 Years MVA	10392	2102	95	32	12622	65431
3 Years MVA	11540	2717	121	36	14413	76332
4 Years MVA	13392	2675	149	43	16259	85269
5 Years MVA	14690	2717	165	46	17617	90662
6 Years MVA	15449	2632	173	47	18300	91854
7 Years MVA	15980	2554	170	44	18747	91852
8 Years MVA	17089	2486	170	43	19788	88978
9 Years MVA	18312	2481	169	42	21004	85128
10 Years MVA	19347	2461	169	42	22019	80610
Average	19347	2461	169	42	22019	80610
CAGR	11.42	2.52	10.88	6.32	10.40	-5.35

Source: Published annual reports of the companies, *Industrial Average*-Performance study of NBFCs by Reserve Bank, *MVA*-Moving Average *CAGR*-Compounded Annual Growth Rate

Table 10 and Times Series Plot 9 reveal the positive linearity in trend as far as investments is concerned. The reasons attributed for this development is higher risk free return in gilt securities and increase in asset financing. This has been vindicated by the high compound annual growth. The risk aversion attitude of management, stringent provisioning

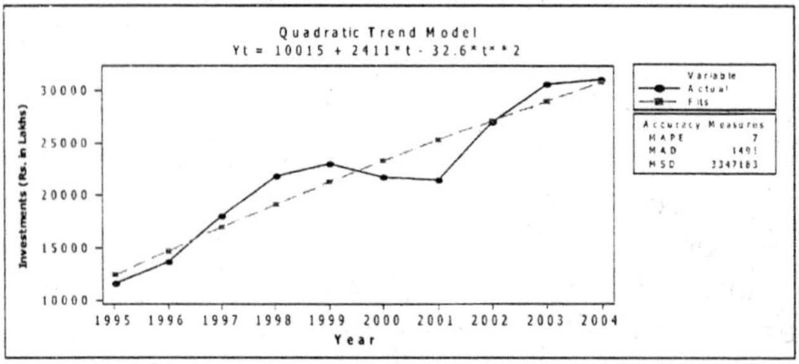

Figure 9 : Plot mapping Trends in Investments of Asset Finance Companies

norms, and statutory maintenance of liquid assets force the linear positive distribution in investment. Further, this period witness increased diversification of business in the areas of insurance, asset management, and mutual fund through new subsidiaries by high profile companies. The asset finance companies with Rs.100 crores of net owned funds are allowed to commence insurance business in joint venture with foreign insurer. The trend has been halted briefly in 2000 and 2001 due to restriction on group exposure and persistence of negative trend in bonds market.

Table 11
Position of Current Assets of Asset Finance Companies

Current Assets (Amount Rupees in Lakhs)						
	Sub Sample					
Sample Data/Year	*Strata I*	*Strata II*	*Strata III*	*Strata IV*	*Sample Total*	*Industrial Average*
2 Years MVA	114779	19061	729	396	134965	443532
3 Years MVA	127905	20663	885	437	149891	519300
4 Years MVA	133574	23356	1096	499	158524	584100
5 Years MVA	133082	25810	1216	489	160597	610672
6 Years MVA	135576	29627	1304	481	166990	618538
7 Years MVA	138983	33281	1360	482	174106	641744
8 Years MVA	135966	36321	1392	486	174166	678259
9 Years MVA	129331	39186	1442	485	170444	676615
10 Years MVA	121407	42446	1492	491	165835	679691
Average	121407	42446	1492	491	165835	679691
CAGR	-7.05	15.25	11.80	6.58	0.17	9.70

Source: Published annual reports of the companies, *Industrial Average*-Performance study of NBFCs by Reserve Bank, *MVA*-Moving Average *CAGR*-Compounded Annual Growth Rate.

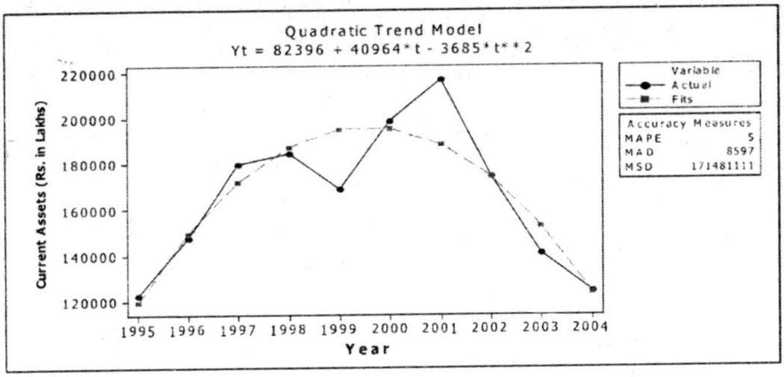

Figure 10 : Plot mapping Trends in Current Assets of Asset Finance Companies

Table 11 and Times Series plot 10 reveal asymmetrical distribution in current asset holding in the form of stock on hire, cash holdings and lease investment. In 1995-96, the holdings in hired assets have increased. The closure of finance companies in 1996 and enactment of stringent asset provisioning norms, and increasing bad debts due to high cost of finance have seriously affected the holdings in current assets from 1998 till 2003. Besides, the banks have diversified the business into leasing and consumer durable financing. Lack of lendable resources for the banks in 2001 due to higher statutory commitments and low cost of finance has given breather for these companies. On whole, the asset financing in the form of hired stock holdings, and leased assets is on the decline. The reason is that the finance companies are resorting to short term financing than long-term risky financing. The asset restructuring through sale of recoverable infuse funds into the companies is main reason for decline in short –term asset holdings. This is, again, vindicated by the fairly low compounded annual growth.

Table 12 and Time Series Plot 11 reveal asymmetrical distribution in holdings in hire purchase finance assets. Till 1999, the banks have been lending to working capital and concentrated more on personal finance. With the booming economy, steady growth in consumer durables, automobile market attracted many banks to venture into asset financing. Due to their low cost of funds raised from diverse sources, the finance charges have been kept low by the bank to gain market share. This has dented the growth of asset financing by the finance companies. Raising cost of operations, limited access to cheaper finance, stringent risk asset provisioning have taken toll on the asset finance companies. Diversification of risk through asset restructuring, sale of assets to asset managers and exploration into new business such as insurance, healthcare, travel management have reduced holdings in leased assets as seen from negative annual compound growth.

Table 12
Position of Stock on Hire of Asset Finance Companies

	Stock on Hire (Amount Rupees in Lakhs)					
	Sub Sample					
Sample Data/Year	*Strata I*	*Strata II*	*Strata III*	*Strata IV*	*Sample Total*	*Industrial Average*
2 Years MVA	106512	15184	570	335	122600	317593
3 Years MVA	118341	16266	632	376	135615	411259
4 Years MVA	122972	18840	864	439	143115	482227
5 Years MVA	123962	21281	1018	428	146690.	518102
6 Years MVA	127192	24857	1123	420	153592	529830
7 Years MVA	131018	28271	1190	425	160903	556488
8 Years MVA	128277	30890	1235	431	160833	591619
9 Years MVA	121821	33084	1297	433	156635	591173
10 Years MVA	113924	35469	1355	441	151189	592240
Average	113924	35469	1355	441	151189	592240
CAGR	-7.36	13.14	13.54	8.54	-0.55	10.12

Source: Published annual reports of the companies, *Industrial Average*-Performance study of NBFCs by Reserve Bank, *MVA*-Moving Average *CAGR*-Compounded Annual Growth Rate.

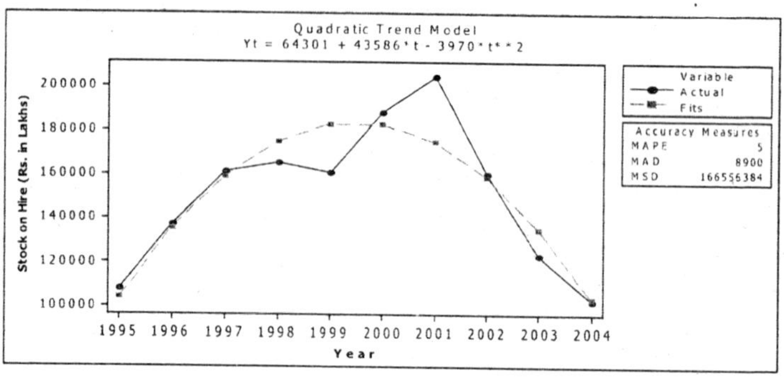

Figure 11: Plot mapping Trends in Stock on Hire of Asset Finance Companies

ANALYSIS OF EARNINGS PROFILE OF ASSET FINANCE COMPANIES IN TAMIL NADU

Table 13
Position of Fee-Based Earnings by Asset Finance Companies

	Fee Income (Amount Rupees in Lakhs)					
	Sub Sample					
Sample Data/Year	*Strata I*	*Strata II*	*Strata III*	*Strata IV*	*Sample Total*	*Industrial Average*
2 Years MVA	1453	0	0	13	1467	213
3 Years MVA	1329	56	0	15	1400	297
4 Years MVA	1281	48	0	13	1343	276
5 Years MVA	1389	58	0	11	1457	263
6 Years MVA	1353	60	0	9	1422	371
7 Years MVA	1540	89	0	9	1637	359
8 Years MVA	1565	115	0	8	1688	357
9 Years MVA	1535	136	0	9	1680	319
10 Years MVA	1536	124	0	9	1669	356
Average	1536	124	0	9	1669	356
CAGR	1.24	0.00	0.00	0.00	1.41	12.13

Source: Published annual reports of the companies, *Industrial Average*-Performance study of NBFCs by Reserve Bank, *MVA*-Moving Average *CAGR*-Compounded Annual Growth Rate.

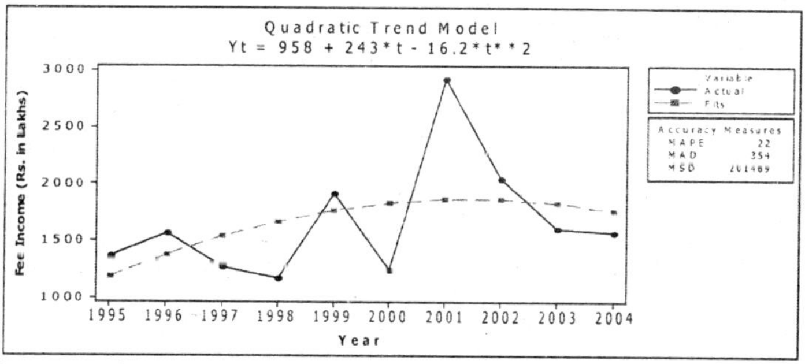

Figure 12: Plot mapping Trends in Fee-Based Earnings of Asset Finance Companies

Table 13 and Time Series plot 12 reveal positive reasonably symmetric distribution in trend. The reasons, they attribute, are the enforcement of strict norms on business activities, limited avenues for business development, high-risk involvement in asset financing, and reduction in exposure to capital market investments due to high incidence of manipulation in secondary market. Increased competition from banks in the funds based financing, relatively reduced risk in fee-based activities such as software development, underwriting of insurance, travel management and health care have forced the asset finance companies to diversify their business into fee-based activities. The legal impediments in enforcing recovery ethics have dented the traditional funds-based activities. Earnings from fee-based activities have been the key focus of management strategy. The dominance of the multinational players, domestic institutions like ICICI has increased due to their advantages of competitive funding costs, support of international parents and sophisticated mechanisms to monitor and control risks. The stiff competition has forced the non-bank finance companies to change their business strategies like shift from traditional fund-based activities to fee-based activities and diversification into new businesses. The change in business strategies has, altogether, affected the earnings in core business sector (Ingres 2006). The negative distribution from 1996-98 has been due to lack of infrastructural facilities and lack of knowledge in fee-based activities. Highly uptrend in 2001 is due to opening of insurance sector, and mutual fund activities to finance companies. The downtrend after 2001 is due to increased competition from banks in the insurance sector, in which the State Bank of India commenced high profile insurance operations through a subsidiary. Further, tourism and travel related services are on downtrend attributable to security issues, communal riots. However, the fee-based activity is holding key for the future business ventures.

Table 14 and Time Series plot 13 reveal the asymmetrical distribution in trend. Till 1999, these companies have not felt the impact of regulations. The impact has been seriously felt in the early 2000, as the fund-based activity is fraught with increased risk and provisioning requirements. The future opportunities will be in rural markets, fund-based activities – financing intangibles such as education, health, travel etc, and the fee-based activities in information technology, infrastructure, and environment sectors (Kshirsagar 2003). The provisioning requirements have caused serious dent on the profitability of the funds-based activities. Further, increased competition from commercial banks with low finance charges, declining market share, non-recoverability and asset stripping, mounting non-performing loans have forced the companies to reduce their funds-based activities. However, the low profile companies continue concentrate on funds-based activities in spite of increased competition due to their personalized customer care, good rapport with customers make it easy to enforce recovery, and their geographical proximity with customers. The reason attributed to negative trend in 1998-2000 is enforcement of provisioning norms. However, the uptrend in 2001 and 2003 is mainly due to high consumption behaviour of the middle class particularly with regard to automobiles and consumer durables. Economic prosperity has created demand for consumer durables in India. Therefore, the opportunities for finance companies are plenty. Besides, the automobile production is driven largely by domestic savings, interest rate, inflation, and tax moderation. (Sharma 2005). The negative downtrend is vindicated by the negative compounded annual growth.

Table 14
Position of Earnings through Funds-Based Activities of Asset Finance Companies

	Funds Income (Amount Rupees in Lakhs)					
	Sub Sample					
Sample Data/Year	*Strata I*	*Strata II*	*Strata III*	*Strata IV*	*Sample Total*	*Industrial Average*
2 Years MVA	25732	10941	292	62	37026	112510
3 Years MVA	29828	11758	348	81	42015	145765
4 Years MVA	32867	12296	387	100	45650	178095
5 Years MVA	34720	12767	409	104	48000	191651
6 Years MVA	35666	13267	410	101	49444	193852
7 Years MVA	37349	13559	409	99	51417	191524
8 Years MVA	37457	13632	407	99	51595	192566
9 Years MVA	37913	13649	409	98	52068	190289
10 Years MVA	37083	13564	413	97	49874	189425
Average	37083	13564	413	97	49874	189425
CAGR	3.05	2.49	8.35	7.06	-0.66	8.08

Source: Published annual reports of the companies, *Industrial Average*-Performance study of NBFCs by Reserve Bank, *MVA*-Moving Average *CAGR*-Compounded Annual Growth Rate

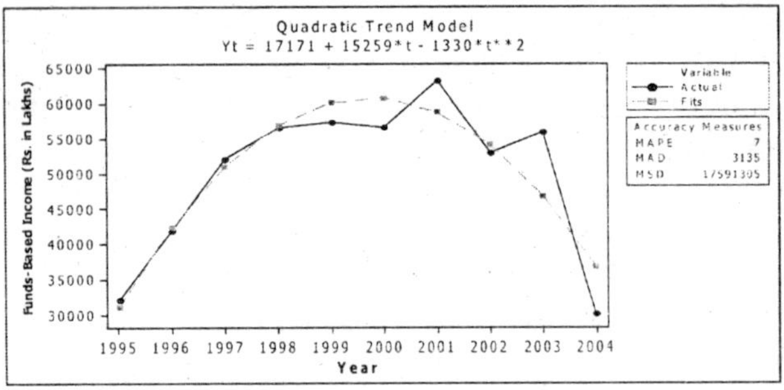

Figure 13 : Plot mapping Trends in Funds-Based Earnings of Asset Finance Companies

Table 15

Position of Lease Income of the Asset Finance Companies

	Lease Rentals (Amount Rupees in Lakhs)					
	Sub Sample					
Sample Data/Year	*Strata I*	*Strata II*	*Strata III*	*Strata IV*	*Sample Total*	*Industrial Average*
2 Years MVA	7710	521	98	5	8333	53205
3 Years MVA	9085	641	140	8	9874	68250
4 Years MVA	10334	630	148	11	11123	76705
5 Years MVA	11536	638	130	12	12317	80461
6 Years MVA	12759	597	111	12	13479	79980
7 Years MVA	13530	642	98	10	14280	75224
8 Years MVA	13991	682	87	9	14769	69995
9 Years MVA	13967	711	78	8	14764	64948
10 Years MVA	12709	697	70	7	13483	60284
Average	12709	697	70	7	13483	60284
CAGR	-13.76	2.90	-100.00	-100.00	-12.38	-7.07

Source: Published annual reports of the companies, *Industrial Average*-Performance study of NBFCs by Reserve Bank, *MVA*-Moving Average *CAGR*-Compounded Annual Growth Rate

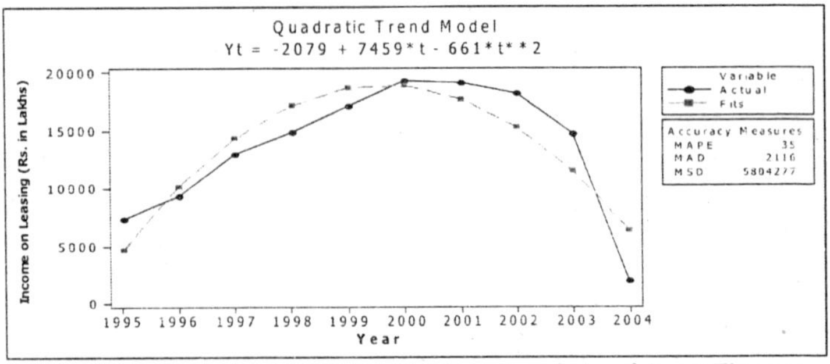

Figure 14 : Plot mapping Trends in Lease Earnings of Asset Finance Companies

Table 15 and time series plot 14 reveal, again, the asymmetrical distribution in trend. Till the impact the regulations, provisioning requirements, increased competition from banks, and the asset finance companies have been enjoying uptrend in leasing business in the initial phase (1995-1999). With the entry of multinationals and banks in asset financing, increasing cost of funds resulting higher finance charges, enhancement of risk profile of asset leasing have seriously affected the lease business profile of asset finance companies. The downtrend is more pronounced in last phase (2001-2004). The asset leasing witness sharp downtrend in 2004 due to higher cost of funds, shift in consumer behaviour from consumption to savings, imposition of service tax on leasing activities. This is, again, proved by high negative compound annual growth. This is forcing the asset finance companies to shun away from asset leasing business.

Table 16
Position of Income on Hire Purchasing Activities of Asset Finance Companies

	Hire Purchase Finance Charges (Amount Rupees in Lakhs)					
	Sub Sample					
Sample Data/Year	*Strata I*	*Strata II*	*Strata III*	*Strata IV*	*Sample Total*	*Industrial Average*
2 Years MVA	18022	10482	194	57	28755	59305
3 Years MVA	20743	11239	236	72	32290	77515
4 Years MVA	22533	11792	282	89	34695	101390
5 Years MVA	23183	12264	315	92	35854	111190
6 Years MVA	22907	12799	330	89	36125	113871
7 Years MVA	23819	13631	338	89	37877	116300
8 Years MVA	23465	14488	344	90	38387	122571
9 Years MVA	23946	14538	353	90	38927	125341
10 Years MVA	24374	14349	362	90	39175	129141
Average	24374	14349	362	90	39175	129141
CAGR	6.49	2.76	11.30	7.31	5.23	13.66

Source: Published annual reports of the companies, *Industrial Average*-Performance study of NBFCs by Reserve Bank, *MVA*-Moving Average *CAGR*-Compounded Annual Growth Rate

Table 16 and Time Series plot 15 reveal symmetrical distribution in trend compared to plot 14. The easy enforcement of hire purchase agreements than leasing is the main reason for the difference in trend. As in the case of leasing, the hire purchase financing is on uptrend till 2000. But with the competition is growing and entry of many new players, shift consumption behaviour, risk aversion of executives have stalled the uptrend. With the hire purchase financing market is becoming more mature, high cost of operations affected the uptrend from 2000. It is observed, from early 2001, that the trend has been on steady downward movement. Increase in the price of Automobiles, Consumer Electronics, and entertainment products are the major causes for the trend. In spite of this, the hire purchase activity has registered healthy 5% annual growth on a compounded basis. The asset finance companies operating on a limited scale are concentrating on hire purchase finance activities.

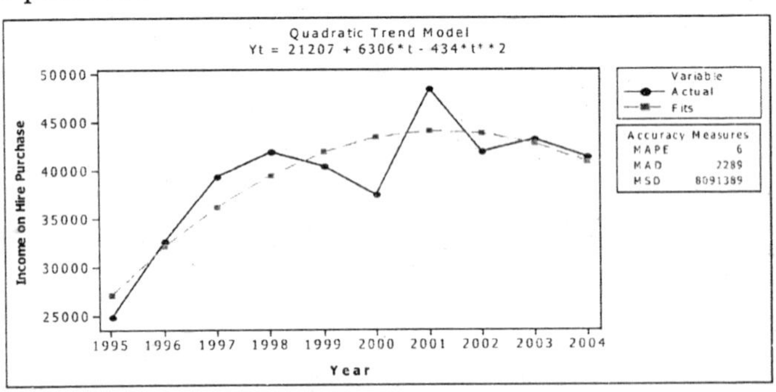

Figure 15 : Plot mapping Trends in HirePurchase Earnings of Asset Finance Companies

Table 17 and Times Series plot 16 reveal more pronounced asymmetrical distribution in trend as far as non-business earnings profile is concerned. Till 2000, these companies' non-business earnings are on uptrend due to high returns in the form of dividends from investments in subsidiaries, interest income from unlisted high yield bonds. With the prescription of group and capital market exposure norms on investments in subsidiaries, and net owned funds requirements, the companies sold substantial holdings in subsidiaries or in capital markets. Besides, the stock market manipulation in 2001 have seriously jeopardized the value of underlying securities.

Capital market financing in the form of public offer finance, loan on securities by the non-banking finance companies has resulted in too much exposure to over-heated stock markets. Therefore, the regulatory restrictions on capital market exposure are a welcome as it reduces the credit and operational risks (Crisil 2006). But with the economy back on track and relaxation of capital market exposure have paved way for increase in earnings from non-business activities.

Table 17
Position of Income on Non-Business Activities of Asset Finance Companies

	Non-Business Income (Amount Rupees in Lakhs)					
	Sub Sample					
Sample Data/Year	*Strata I*	*Strata II*	*Strata III*	*Strata IV*	*Sample Total*	*Industrial Average*
2 Years MVA	1453	0	0	13	1467	213
2 Years MVA	1533	1126	20	6	2685	12393
3 Years MVA	1777	1142	24	10	2954	14415
4 Years MVA	1892	1212	30	13	3147	17134
5 Years MVA	1978	1304	33	15	3329	18303
6 Years MVA	2132	1249	32	15	3428	17928
7 Years MVA	1905	1199	31	15	3149	17533
8 Years MVA	2222	1153	30	14	3419	17392
9 Years MVA	2108	1096	30	13	3247	17902
10 Years MVA	2012	1069	30	14	3125	17607
Average	2012	1069	30	14	3125	17607
CAGR	-2.21	-1.71	10.94	20.44	-1.81	3.30

Source: Published annual reports of the companies, *Industrial Average*-Performance study of NBFCs by Reserve Bank, *MVA*-Moving Average *CAGR*-Compounded Annual Growth Rate.

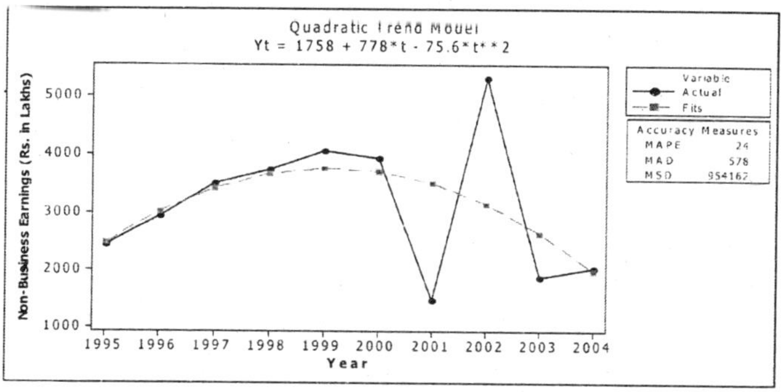

Figure 16 : Plot mapping Trends in Non-Business Earnings of Asset Finance Companies

ANALYSIS OF EXPENSE PROFILE OF ASSET FINANCE COMPANIES

Table 18
Position of Interest Cost on the Fixed Loan of the Asset Finance Companies

	Interest - Fixed Loans (Amount Rupees in Lakhs)					
	Sub Sample					
Sample Data/Year	*Strata I*	*Strata II*	*Strata III*	*Strata IV*	*Sample Total*	*Industrial Average*
2 Years MVA	9873	3322	122	33	13351	56699
3 Years MVA	12764	3734	158	48	16704	73704
4 Years MVA	14247	3851	195	58	18352	89363
5 Years MVA	14703	3922	218	62	18905	98568
6 Years MVA	14605	3921	232	60	18818	101084
7 Years MVA	14424	4168	240	58	18890	98892
8 Years MVA	14288	4443	246	57	19033	101290
9 Years MVA	14109	4520	253	56	18939	100814
10 Years MVA	13840	4505	259	55	18659	99675
Average	13840	4505	259	55	18659	99675
CAGR	3.47	3.52	15.24	9.10	3.63	8.01

Source: Published annual reports of the companies, *Industrial Average*-Performance study of NBFCs by Reserve Bank, *MVA*-Moving Average *CAGR*-Compounded Annual Growth Rate.

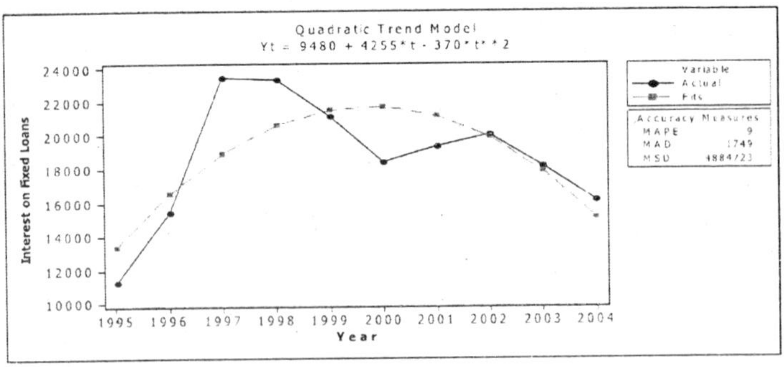

Figure 17 : Plot mapping Trends in Interst Costs of Asset Finance Companies

Table 18 and Time Series plot 17 reveal asymmetrical distribution in trend in interest burden faced by asset finance companies. The interest burden has been quite high till 1999. The reasons are higher interest paid for public deposits to attract them in the face of competition from banks, and to arrest the outflow in the wake of failure of quite a number of finance companies. From 2000, the cost of funds is coming down due to low inflation, moderation in real interest rates, flexible interest rate regime promoted by Reserve Bank of India are main reason for declining cost of funds. The focus of the Indian government on moderation of interest tax and virtual abolition has led to reduced cost of finance. The interest burden for asset finance companies has drastically increased in 1997-98 due to higher inflation coupled with heavy competition from banks. We confirm that the GDP growth influences the earnings of the Non Banking Finance Companies in a significant way. Lower GDP does not mean higher earnings; the results only suggest that the GDP should not show divergence over the period (Thiyagarajan 2004a). According to Lo, "...the economic prosperity and low inflation will give a push effect to the economic units viz., private and public sector units and translates in the growth of profits and in other financial measures..." (Lo, Andrew 1984). During 2000, the downtrend in interest cost is more pronounced as the Reserve Bank reduced the Statutory Liquidity requirements for the banks, which pumped more funds into the financial sector. However, the compounded annual growth of interest burden is in positive side causing concern for the executives. Low inflation in 2004 accounts for the sharp decline in the burden.

Table 19 and Times Series plot 18 reveal the staff cost is exhibiting fairly linear distribution with steady growth. The reasons for increase in staff cost are increase in cost of living, higher economic growth; salary increases prevalent in the sector as well as across the industries. Besides, new business ventures require more staffing. Staffing cost, administrative cost that can be controlled is on the rise due to trends in intra-industry and inter-industry (Khan 2002). The geographical diversification results in higher staffing requirements. The reasons attributed for higher staffing are initial service promotional activities, strengthening recovery mechanism, and inflationary pressures. From 2000-2002, the staff related expenditure has declined substantially through introduction of voluntary retirement scheme, redeployment of excess staff to new business activities.

Table 19
Position of Staff Cost incurred by Asset Finance Companies

	Staff Salary (Amount Rupees in Lakhs)					
	Sub Sample					
Sample Data/Year	*Strata I*	*Strata II*	*Strata III*	*Strata IV*	*Sample Total*	*Industrial Average*
2 Years MVA	659	86	15	11	772	3291
3 Years MVA	732	108	18	21	879	4234
4 Years MVA	822	115	22	29	988	5106
5 Years MVA	915	128	24	32	1098	5974
6 Years MVA	987	129	25	32	1173	6576
7 Years MVA	1065	145	26	32	1269	6894
8 Years MVA	1141	163	27	33	1364	7180
9 Years MVA	1279	178	28	33	1518	7364
10 Years MVA	1425	191	29	33	1679	7612
Average	1425	191	29	33	1679	7612
CAGR	16.94	13.56	12.64	25.52	16.68	15.10

Source: Published annual reports of the companies, *Industrial Average*-Performance study of NBFCs by Reserve Bank, *MVA*-Moving Average *CAGR*-Compounded Annual Growth Rate

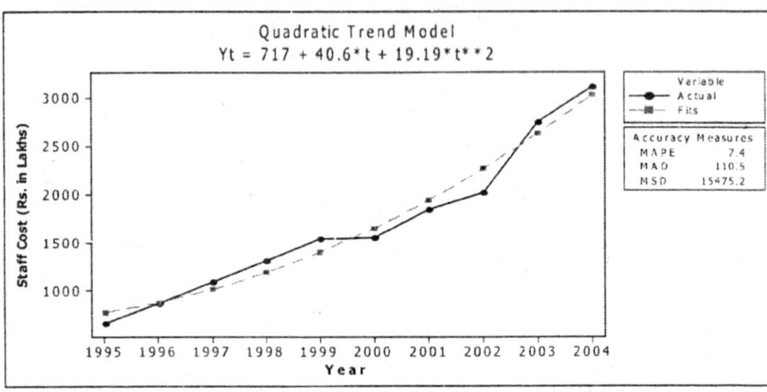

Figure 18 : Plot mapping Trends in Staff Cost of Asset Finance Companies

Table 20 and Times Series plot 19 reveal quite interestingly symmetrical though, the provisioning requirements have increased, and the actual provisioning is in asymmetrical distribution. The negative trend exhibited in this statutory requirement is mainly due to earlier higher provision for bad loans and strengthened recovery mechanism resulting in higher collection of receivables and bad debts. In the initial phase (1995-1997), the provisioning has been adopted to a limited extent and norms have not been rigid. The sharp

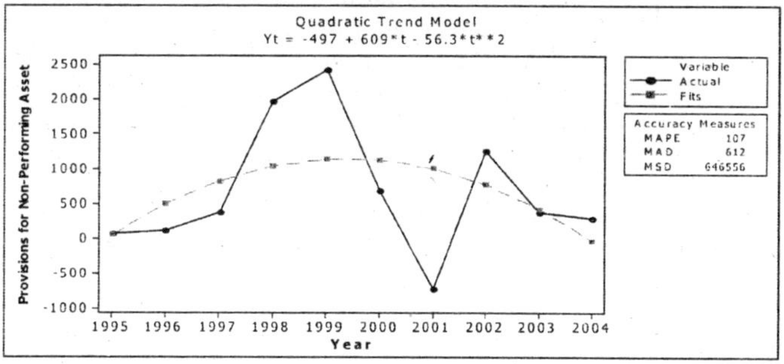

Figure 19: Plot mapping Trends in NPA Provisions of Asset Finance Companies

uptrend in 1998 to 1999 is attributed to introduction current regulatory framework on risk management and strict vigil kept by the Reserve Bank of India. The statutory framework is helpful in recovering the non-performing assets, provided host of other things are put into place (Saha Kausick 2003). However, the downtrend has been perceptible during 2000-01 due to strengthened recovery mechanism, lower disbursements, and sound credit appraisal and post sanction follow-up. The risks faced by the finance companies emanates from fund-based activities rather than executive defaults (Crisil 2006). Measuring and managing credit risk has become core for financial institutions. In most countries, banks' equity requirements are already tied to their exposure to credit risk. (Dangl 2003). In recent years (2002 to 2004), the trend is upward with the inflationary pressures exert pressure on customer to spend more to meet their livelihood needs, low domestic saving resulting in mounting non-performing loans. However, the compounded annual growth reveals the overall position is negative. Jimenez focused on limited set of determinants (collateral, type of lender and bank- borrower relationship), while controlling for the other explanatory variables such as the macroeconomic environment, characteristics of the borrower and of the loan (instrument, currency, maturity and size) and supported the viewpoint that collateral might decrease the screening efforts by banks for probable default but the same increases ex post probability of default of loan (Jimenez, 2004).

Table 20
Position of Provisioning for Non-Performing Assets of Asset Finance Companies

	Provisioning Expenses (Amount Rupees in Lakhs)					
	Sub Sample					
Sample Data/Year	*Strata I*	*Strata II*	*Strata III*	*Strata IV*	*Sample Total*	*Industrial Average*
2 Years MVA	33	53	1	0	87	1479
3 Years MVA	94	86	6	0	186	1661
4 Years MVA	438	182	14	1	635	3030
5 Years MVA	780	192	16	8	996	3617
6 Years MVA	678	238	14	17	946	4387
7 Years MVA	381	289	13	24	707	4373
8 Years MVA	388	355	12	22	777	5765
9 Years MVA	326	375	11	20	732	5772
10 Years MVA	301	372	11	18	688	5307
Average	301	372	11	18	688	5307
CAGR	1.36	57.07	23.71	0.00	15.44	3.85

Source: Published annual reports of the companies, *Industrial Average*-Performance study of NBFCs by Reserve Bank, *MVA*-Moving Average *CAGR*-Compounded Annual Growth Rate.

ANALYSIS OF RETURNS GENERATED BY ASSET FINANCE COMPANIES

Table 21
Position of Profit from Core Operating Activities of Asset Finance Companies

	Core Operating Profit After Tax (Amount Rupees in Lakhs)					
	Sub Sample					
Sample Data/Year	*Strata I*	*Strata II*	*Strata III*	*Strata IV*	*Sample Total*	*Industrial Average*
2 Years MVA	4313	960	67	3	5342	1265
3 Years MVA	4511	1078	65	1	5655	3012
4 Years MVA	5277	1131	60	1	6470	5880
5 Years MVA	5701	1094	55	1	6850	7785
6 Years MVA	5981	1334	45	1	7360	4502
7 Years MVA	7311	1518	40	2	8871	4648
8 Years MVA	7136	1645	36	2	8819	4140
9 Years MVA	7410	1737	33	3	9182	3905
10 Years MVA	7373	1795	31	1	9200	4698
Average	7373	1795	31	1	9200	4698
CAGR	6.45	8.04	-12.01	83.46	6.69	12.35

Source: Published annual reports of the companies, *Industrial Average*-Performance study of NBFCs by Reserve Bank, *MVA*- Moving Average *CAGR*-Compounded Annual Growth Rate.

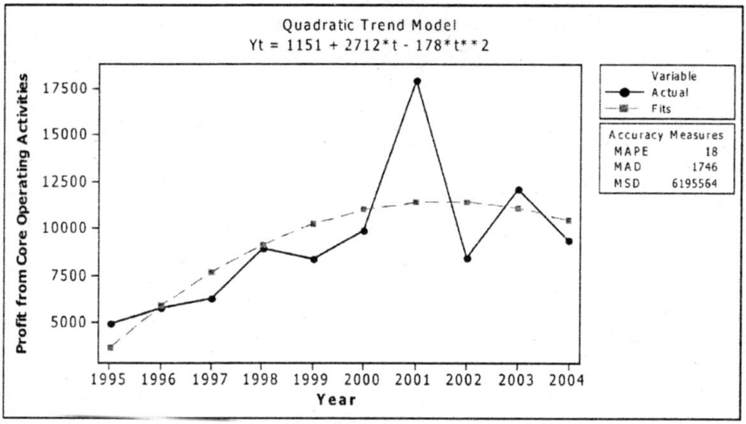

Figure 20 : Plot mapping Trends in Core Profit of Asset Finance Companies

Table 21 and Times Series plot 20 reveal the asymmetrical distribution in trend. The reasons for share decline in profit generated from core business activities is decline in the core business, viz., leasing and hire purchase finance, decrease in core business expenditure viz., administrative expenses, interest burden, and to a small extent staff compensation. Low inflation coupled with higher utilization of infrastructure, easy access to cheap finance during 1997 & 1999, control of other expenditures are the major reasons attributed to the trend. However, strict vigil has to be maintained on the cost side as it can adversely affect the profitability of these companies.

Table 22 and Times Series plot 21 reveal imperfect positively symmetrical distribution in trend. The cash generated from operations are increasing in 1996-1998 mainly due to increase in funds-based activities. Core operations show positive skewness during this period. Lease disbursements are more pronounced in that period than in other period. Moreover, easier cash credit accommodation provided by the banks has aided increase in cash flow generation from operations. During 1999-2000, the downtrend in cash flow is more pronounced and is due to lower disbursement and mounting receivables, sale of non-business assets with reduced earnings are also attributes for this trend.

Table 22
Position of Cash Generated from Operations of Asset Finance Companies

	Operating Cash Flow (Amount Rupees in Lakhs)					
	Sub Sample					
Sample Data/Year	*Strata I*	*Strata II*	*Strata III*	*Strata IV*	*Sample Total*	*Industrial Average*
2 Years MVA	6436	1011	45	8	7500	17199
3 Years MVA	6685	1498	60	11	8254	25436
4 Years MVA	7156	1640	58	11	8865	31684
5 Years MVA	7087	1811	63	8	8968	24516
6 Years MVA	6997	1883	60	5	8946	13752
7 Years MVA	7468	1964	61	6	9499	15578
8 Years MVA	7768	2034	60	4	9866	13851
9 Years MVA	8237	2075	60	3	10376	15475
10 Years MVA	8560	1867	60	2	10489	17250
Average	8560	1867	60	2	10489	17250
CAGR	7.05	0	0	0	6.72	0

Source: Published annual reports of the companies, *Industrial Average*-Performance study of NBFCs by Reserve Bank, *MVA*-Moving Average *CAGR*-Compounded Annual Growth Rate.

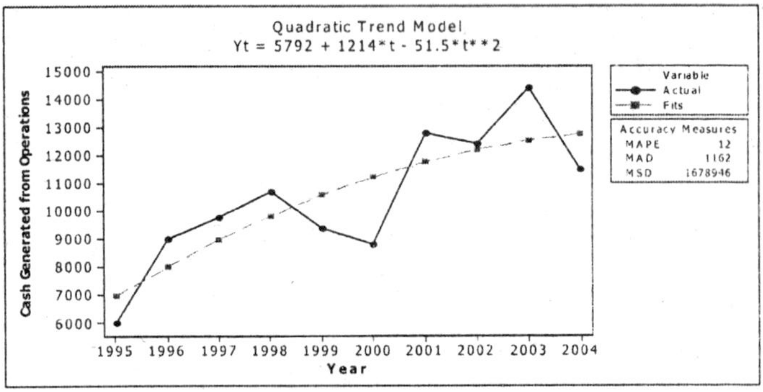

Figure 21 : Plot mapping Trends in Operational Cash of Asset Finance Companies

Table 23 and Time Series plot 22 reveal near-linear negative trend. The competition from banks and financial institutions in core business activities, increased cost of funds, higher tax liability, high incidence of bad debts, increase in non-business expenditure are the major causes for persistence of the trend. Lending to micro-finance sector, viz., self-help groups is much more profitable and lowers the scope of the risk provisioning. The finance companies, through micro-finance, can increase their earnings (Ananth Bindu 2004). The pronounced downtrend in 2000 is mainly due to high inflation, economic growth driving high cost of funds, reduced business from stiff competition from banks with huge funds on relaxation of liquidity requirements. Given this feature, an increase in the rate of inflation drives down the real rate of return not just on money, but also on assets in general. The implied reduction in real returns exacerbates credit market frictions (Boyd J 2000). The severe squeeze experienced by finance companies on their operating as well as net margins can be attributed to high cost of debt, increase in operating expenses, low productivity and slow absorption of technology (Kshirsagar 2003). The downtrend is arrested in 2004 mainly due to reduced staff cost, control of expenditure, low-cost fee-based activities, positive inflation, easy access to cheap financing sources, high retention of earnings, and finally flexible interest regime.

Table 23
Position of Return Earned for Common Equity of Asset Finance Companies

	Return on Equity					
	Sub Sample					
Sample Data/Year	*Strata I*	*Strata II*	*Strata III*	*Strata IV*	*Sample Total*	*Industrial Average*
2 Years MVA	29	21	23	5	20	14
3 Years MVA	27	18	21	6	18	13
4 Years MVA	26	17	19	5	17	12
5 Years MVA	24	16	18	3	15	9
6 Years MVA	22	15	16	-1	13	4
7 Years MVA	21	15	15	0	13	5
8 Years MVA	19	14	14	0	12	3
9 Years MVA	18	14	13	-1	11	4
10 Years MVA	18	13	13	-1	11	4
Average	18	13	13	-1	11	4
CAGR	-9.66	-11.63	-11.77	-5.77	-12.16	-2.56

Source: Published annual reports of the companies, *Industrial Average*-Performance study of NBFCs by Reserve Bank, *MVA*-Moving Average *CAGR*-Compounded Annual Growth Rate

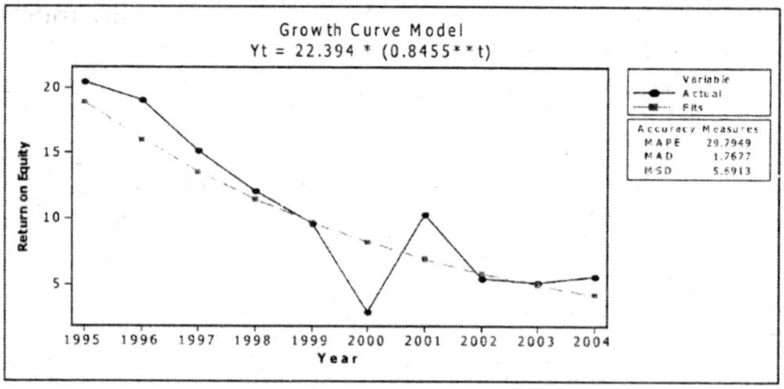

Figure 22 : Plot mapping Trends in Return on Equity of Asset Finance Companies

STRUCTURAL EQUATION MODEL FOR ASSET FINANCE COMPANIES FOR CREATION OF SHARE HOLDERS' WEALTH

In hierarchical regression, the predictor variables are entered in sets of variables according to a pre-determined order that may infer some causal or potentially mediating relationships between the predictors and the dependent variables (Francis, 2003). Such situations are frequently of interest in the social sciences. The logic involved in hypothesizing mediating relationships is that "the independent variable influences the mediator which, in turn, influences the outcome" (Holmbeck, 1997). However, an important pre-condition for examining mediated relationships is that the independent variable is significantly associated with the dependent variable prior to testing any model for mediating variables (Holmbeck, 1997). Of interest is the extent to which the introduction of the hypothesized mediating variable reduces the magnitude of any direct influence of the independent variable on the dependent variable.

Hence, the author empirically tested the hierarchical regression for the models of *BEM – ESW (NW), Profit–Cost, TEM-AFC, Profit–ESW*(NW), and ESW-*Income (Deflator)* within the *AMOS* graphics environment.

Regression Model for BEM-ESW (NW)

The path diagram for the hypothesized mediated model is given in the path diagram (see Figure 23).

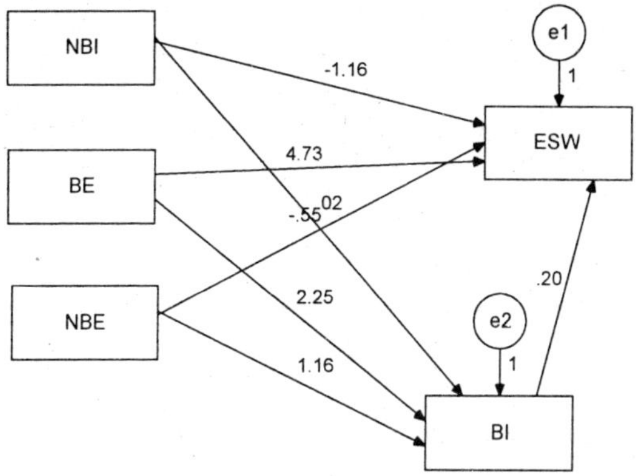

Figure 23 : BEM- ESW (NW) Model

The regression analysis reveals the business earnings. The Non-Business Income -=1.16, followed by Business Expenses= 4.73, Non-Business Expenses = -0.55. The R^2 value of 0.20 for mediating factor. The visual representation of the results suggest that the relationship between dimensions of business and mediated factor. The *NBI* resulted significant impact on mediated factor, Business Income. The *BE* and *NBE* resulted not significant impact on mediated factor, *BI*. It shows that *BE, NBE* not influenced in Equity Shareholders' Wealth. This model represents Asset Finance Companies may concentrate on increasing *BI* and *NBI* for wealth creation..

Posterior Diagnostic Plots of BEM-ESW (NW) Mediated Regression Model

To check the convergence of Bayesian MCMC method the posterior diagnostic plots are analyzed. The following figure (Figures 24) shows the posterior frequency polygon of the distribution of the parameters across the 50,000 samples. The Bayesian MCMC is diagnostic plot reveals that for all the figures the normality is achieved, so the structural equation model fit is accurately estimated

To determine how long it takes for the correlation among the samples to die down, autocorrelation plot which is the estimated correlation between the sampled value at any

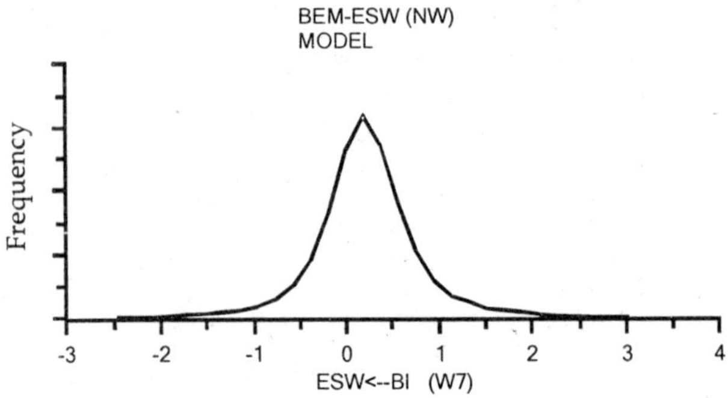

Figure 24 : Posterior Frequency Polygon Distribution of the Business Income and Shareholders' Wealth, Regression Weight (W7)

iteration and the sampled value k iterations later for k = 1,2,3,....is analyzed for *BEM-ESW(NW)*. The figure 25 shows the correlation plot of the *BEM-ESW (NW)* for the mediated factor of Business Income with other dimensions across 50,000 samples. The figures exhibits that the lag 35 and beyond, the correlation is effectively 0. This indicated that by 80 iterations, the MCMC procedure has essentially forgotten its starting position. Forgetting the starting position is equivalent to convergence in distribution. Hence, it is ensured that convergence in distribution is attained, and that the analysis samples are indeed samples from the true posterior distribution

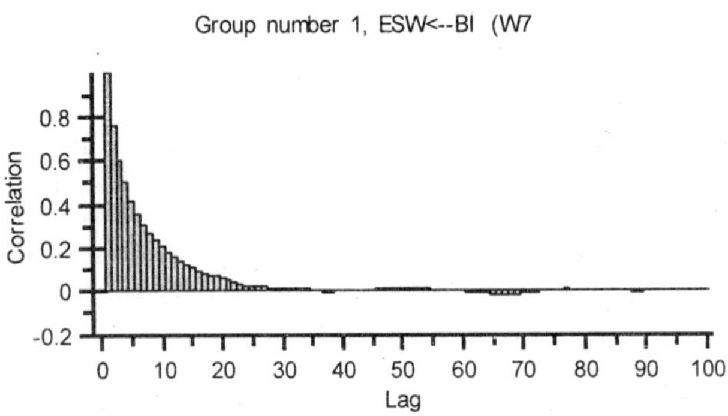

Figure 25 : Posterior Distribution of Autocorrelation among Shareholders' Wealth and Business Income, Regression Weight (W7)

The trace plot also called time series plot shows the sampled values of a parameter over time. This plot helps to judge how quickly the MCMC procedure converges in distribution. The following figure (Figure 26) shows the trace plot of *BEM-ESW (NW)* model for the mediated factor Business Income with other dimensions of business across 50,000 samples. The figure exhibits rapid up and down variation with no long-term trends or drifts. This indicates that the convergence in distribution takes place quickly.

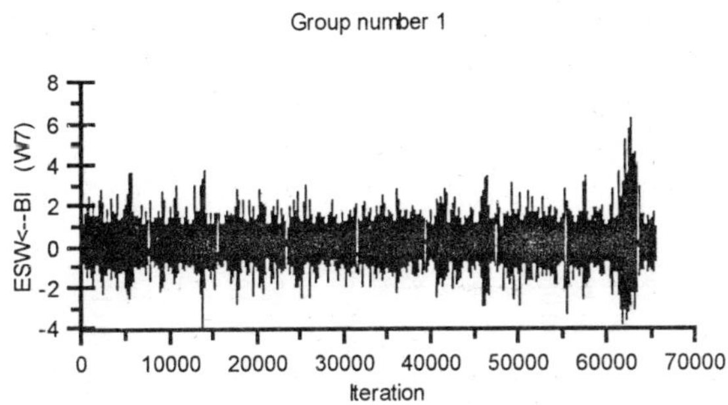

Figure 26 : Posterior Trace Plot of the ESW-NW Model for The Mediated Factor Shareholders' Wealth and Business Income, Regression Weight (W7)

The research model *BEM-ESW (NW)*, while many management scientists are most familiar with the estimation of these models using software that analyses (e.g., LISREL, AMOS), the author adopt Bayesian approach for estimation and inference in AMOS 16.0 environment. Since it offers numerous methodological and substantive advantages over alternative approaches. The table 24 shows the Bayesian convergence distribution of *BEM-ESW (NW)* mediated regression model. In this work, the author has adopted for the procedure of assessing convergence of MCMC (Markov Chain Monte Carlo) algorithm of maximum likelihood. To estimate the MCMC convergence, the author adopted two methods namely, convergence in distribution , convergence of posterior summaries. The values of posterior means accurately estimate the *BEM-ESW (NW)* mediated *SEM* model. From the above

Table 24
Bayesian Convergence Distribution for ESW-NW and Business Income

	Mean	*S.E.*	*S.D.*	*C.S.*	*Skewness*	*Kurtosis*	*Min*	*Max*	*Name*
Regression Weights									
BI<—NBI	-0.014	0.043	5.679	1.00	-0.048	4.208	-49.716	46.113	W1
BI<—BE	2.243	0.016	2.967	1.00	-0.044	4.018	-20.085	26.158	W2
BI<—NBE	1.221	0.058	6.857	1.00	0.012	4.230	-67.488	50.864	W3
ESW<—NBE	-0.494	0.057	5.050	1.00	0.189	4.923	-39.061	42.727	W4
ESW<—BE	4.724	0.024	2.573	1.00	-0.088	4.895	-14.391	24.262	W5
ESW<—NBI	-1.194	0.035	4.071	1.00	-0.057	4.449	-32.211	32.590	W6
ESW<—BI	0.202	0.003	0.618	1.00	-0.079	5.643	-4.868	6.182	W7
Means									
NBI	2343.19	1.573	376.277	1.00	-0.004	2.181	1193.97	5671.951	
BE	7543.52	2.270	590.155	1.00	0.058	2.697	2527.05	12903.53	
NBE	735.216	1.187	339.033	1.00	-0.055	4.294	2894.73	4697.975	
Intercepts									
BI	21319.1	154.72	27542.78	1.00	0.027	4.204	-202317	244466.5	
ESW	-6285.48	199.15	23862.01	1.00	0.137	5.390	-212904	240188.8	
Variances									
NBI	1292038	21627	1204007	1.00	5.751	66.00	174531	30158462	
BE	3118966	34327	2979918	1.00	5.268	47.26	387818	58769048	
NBE	1038659	589502	1331681	1.00	10.131	152.7	128761	32706524	
e2	7700082	390026	94692056	1.00	3.555	16.85	3792675	95538336	
e1	4050570	298574	53608164	1.00	3.196	14.02	1433383	58116339	

table the highest value of Convergence Statistics (C.S) is 1.00 which is less than the 1.002 conservative measure (Gelman et al, 2004). Hence, the author concludes the asset finance companies in non-banking finance sector could concentrate on business income and non-business income partially influences creation of shareholder's wealth in Tamil Nadu. With the help of this regression model, any new entrepreneur could start a business of asset financing by applying this model for creating his own wealth.

REGRESSION MODEL OF THE PROFIT–COST MEDIATED STRUCTURAL EQUATION MODEL

The path diagram for the hypothesized mediated model is given in the path diagram (see Figure 30).

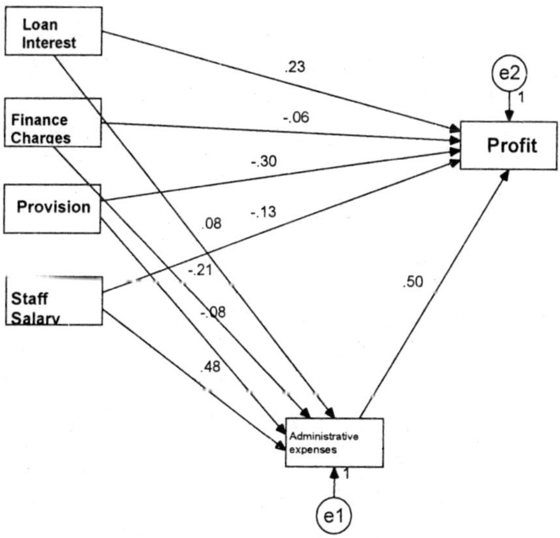

Figure 27 : Profit-Cost Model

The regression analysis in Figure 27 reveals the cost control. The Interest on Loans 0.08, followed by Finance Charges -0.21, Provisioning Expenses -0.08, Staff Salary 0.48. The R^2 value of 0.50 for mediating factor. The visual representation of the results suggest that the relationship between dimensions of

Expenditure and mediated factor. The Loan Interest, Staff Salary, Provisioning Expenses, and Finance Charges resulted significant impact on mediated factor, Administrative Expenses. This model represents Asset Finance Companies may concentrate more on controlling Administrative Expenses and Staff Salary Expenses , besides concentrating on Loan Interest, Provisioning Expenses, and Finance Charges for reporting reasonable profit. The key cost factor to be controlled is Administrative Expenses as otherwise the companies are in maximum likelihood report negative results.

Posterior Diagnostic Plots of Profit – Cost Mediated Regression Model

To check the convergence of Bayesian MCMC method the posterior diagnostic plots are analyzed. The following figure (Figures 28) shows the posterior frequency polygon of the distribution of the parameters across the 50,000 samples. The Bayesian MCMC is diagnostic plot reveals that for all the figures the normality is achieved, so the structural equation model fit is accurately estimated

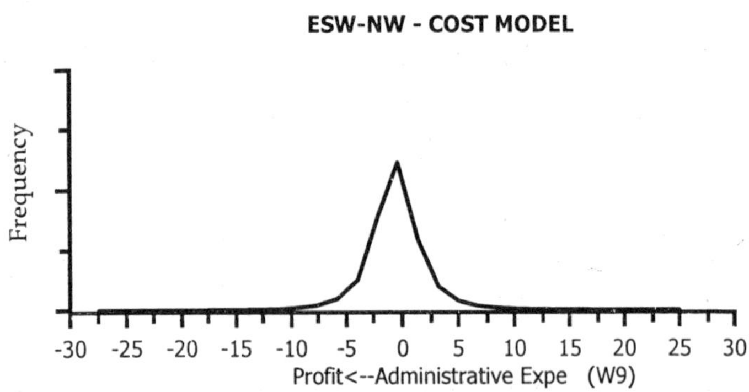

Figure 28 : Posterior Frequesncy Polygon Distribution of the Administrative Expenses and Profitability, Regression Weight (W9)

To determine how long it takes for the correlation among the samples to die down, autocorrelation plot which is the estimated correlation between the sampled value at any iteration and the sampled value k iterations later for k = 1,2,3,....is analyzed for *Profit–Cost Model.* The figure 29 shows the correlation plot of the *Profit–Cost* for the mediated factor of Business Income with other dimensions across 50,000 samples. The figure exhibits that the lag 40 and beyond, the correlation is effectively 0. This indicates that by 80 iterations, the MCMC procedure has essentially forgotten its starting position. Forgetting the starting position is equivalent to convergence in distribution. Hence, it is ensured that convergence in distribution is attained, and that the analysis samples are indeed samples from the true posterior distribution

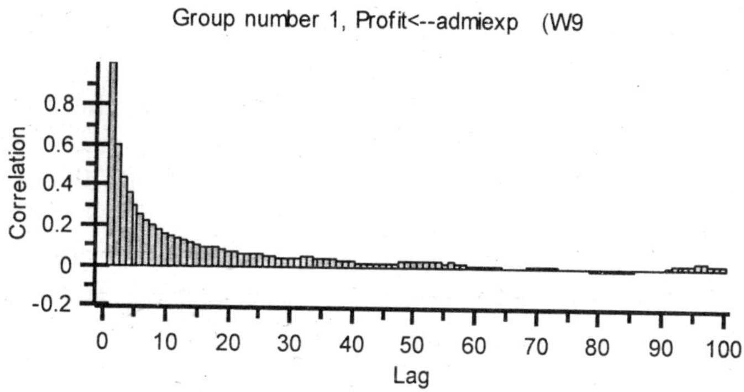

Figure 29 : Posterior Distribution of Autocorrelation among Profitability and Adminexpenses

The trace plot also called time series plot shows the sampled values of a parameter over time. This plot helps to

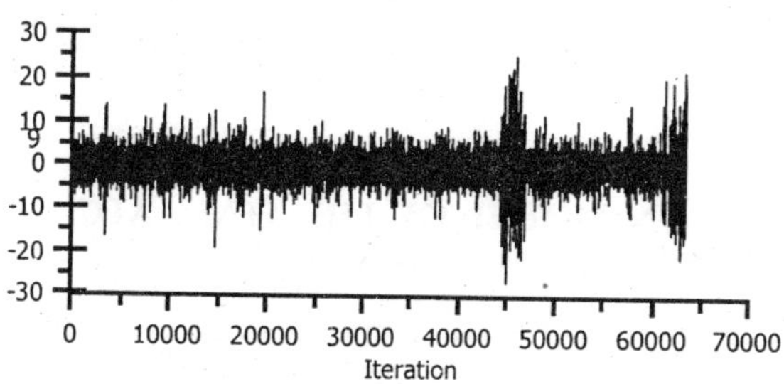

Figure 30 : Posterior Trace Plot of the ESW-NW Model for the Mediated Factor Administrative Expenses and Profitability, Regression Weight (W9)

judge how quickly the MCMC procedure converges in distribution. The following figure (Figure 30) shows the trace plot of *Profit–Cost* model for the mediated factor Administrative Expenses with other dimensions of business across 60,000 samples. The figure exhibits rapid up and down variation with no long-term trends or drifts. This indicates that the convergence in distribution takes place quickly.

The research model *Profit–Cost*, while many management scientists are most familiar with the estimation of these models using software that analyses (e.g., LISREL, AMOS), the author adopt Bayesian approach for estimation and inference in AMOS 16.0 environment. Since it offers numerous methodological and substantive advantages over alternative approaches. The table 25 shows the Bayesian convergence distribution of *Profit–Cost* mediated regression model. In this research, the author has adopted for the procedure of assessing convergence of MCMC (Markov Chain Monte Carlo) algorithm of maximum likelihood. To estimate the MCMC convergence, the author adopted two methods namely, convergence in distribution, convergence of posterior summaries. The values of posterior means accurately estimate the *Profit–Cost* mediated SEM model. From the above table the highest value of Convergence Statistics (C.S) is 1.00, which is less than the 1.002 conservative measures (Gelman et al, 2004). This model explains profit – cost method for asset finance companies in non-banking finance sector. This model scientifically reveals administrative expenses is the core expenses for conducting asset financing business. The entrepreneurs could control administrative expenses (Loan interest, financial charges, provisions and staff salary) for profitability and wealth creation.

REGRESSION MODEL OF THE TEM - AFC MEDIATED STRUCTURAL EQUATION MODEL

The path diagram for the hypothesized mediated model is given in the path diagram (see Figure 31).

The regression analysis reveals the Gross Earnings. The Interest Income -0.17, followed by Dividend Income 0.29, Lease

Table 25
Bayesian Convergence Distribution for ESW-NW Administrative Expenses and Profitability

	Mean	*S.E.*	*S.D.*	*C.S.*	*Skewness*	*Kurtosis*	*Min*	*Max*	*Name*
Regression Weights									
Profit<—Loaninteres	0.234	0.004	0.455	1.000	-0.171	7.221	4.558	5.111	W1
Profit<—Fincharge	-0.069	0.015	1.282	1.000	-0.200	7.051	13.69	12.438	W2
Profit<—Provsion	-0.292	0.007	1.500	1.000	0.030	6.034	16.38	13.586	W3
Profit<—staffsalary	-0.126	0.030	2.644	1.000	-0.147	6.924	25.33	23.491	W4
admiexp<—staffsalary	0.483	0.005	0.711	1.000	0.172	7.091	6.149	8.280	W5
admiexp<—Provsion	-0.080	0.002	0.481	1.000	0.109	8.746	6.090	6.785	W6
admiexp<—Fincharge	-0.208	0.003	0.360	1.000	0.130	7.026	3.904	3.595	W7
admiexp<Loaninteres	0.079	0.001	0.124	1.000	-0.037	7.271	1.238	1.469	W8
Profit<—admiexp	-0.512	0.012	2.840	1.000	-0.097	6.143	27.36	25.010	W9
Means									
Loaninteres	18652.7	7.123	1576.448	1.000	0.008	1.831	6134	35428.219	
Fincharge	2774.10	2.251	744.207	1.000	0.016	1.921	3112	10598.789	
Provsion	685.488	1.213	401.443	1.000	-0.024	1.610	311.3	4004.297	
staffsalary	1678.51	1.164	332.907	1.000	0.006	1.840	1280.	4077.446	
Intercepts									
Profit	6022.71	164.968	13003.9	1.000	0.161	6.620	11327	145886.87	
admiexp	2269.87	25.074	3560.429	1.000	-0.107	6.562	37207	40923.512	
Variances									
Loaninteres	248365	132923	19630603	1.000	4.868	50.014	34204	48171414	
Fincharge	553506	22021	4320047	1.000	4.125	31.178	78441	83692240.	
Provsion	161699	4445	1215315	1.000	4.063	35.846	24526	30691442.	
staffsalary	111436	9106	937312	1.000	7.242	126.05	15971	30930276	
e1	117354	93430	1878068	1.001	5.847	49.198	41719	29105674.	
e2	11620	116227	1697620	1.001	3.653	18.237	32059	16378131	

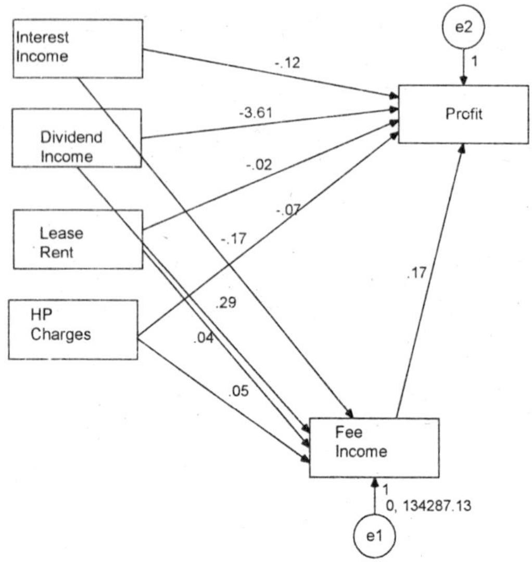

Figure 31 : TEM-AFC Model

Rent 0.04, Hire Purchase Finance Income 0.05. The R^2 value of 0.17 for mediating factor. The visual representation of the results suggest that the relationship between dimensions of Earnings and mediated factor. The Dividend Income, Lease Rent, Hire Purchase Finance Income, Interest Income resulted significant impact on mediated factor, Fee Income. This model represents Asset Finance Companies may concentrate on Fee Income and Interest income for sustainability of profits.

Posterior Diagnostic Plots of BEM-ESW (NW) Mediated Regression Model

To determine how long it takes for the correlation among the samples to die down, autocorrelation plot which is the estimated correlation between the sampled value at any iteration and the sampled value k iterations later for k = 1,2,3,....is analysed for TEM-AFC. The figure 32 shows the correlation plot of the TEM – AFC for the mediated factor of Business Income with other dimensions across 50,000 samples. The figures exhibits that the lag 100 and beyond, the correlation is effectively zero. This indicated that by 80 iterations, the

MCMC procedure has essentially forgotten its starting position. Forgetting the starting position is equivalent to convergence in distribution. Hence, it is ensured that convergence in distribution is attained, and that the analysis samples are indeed samples from the true posterior distribution.

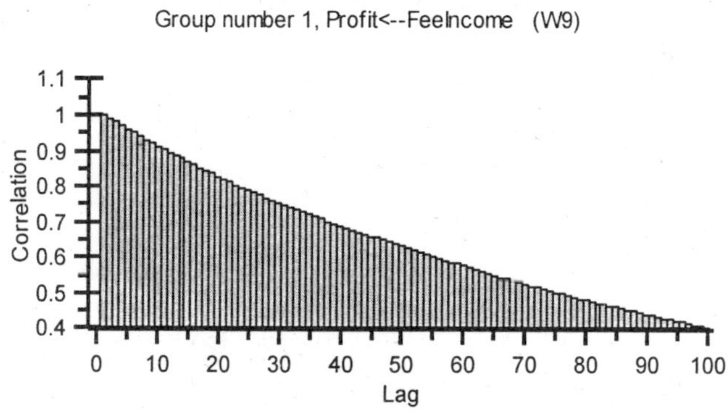

Figure 32 : Posterior Distribution of Autocorrelation among Profitability and Fee-Based Income, Regression Weight (W9)

To check the convergence of Bayesian MCMC method the posterior diagnostic plots are analyzed. The following figure (Figures 33) shows the posterior frequency polygon of the distribution of the parameters across the 50,000 samples. The Bayesian MCMC is diagnostic plot reveals that for all the figures the normality is achieved, so the structural equation model fit is accurately estimated

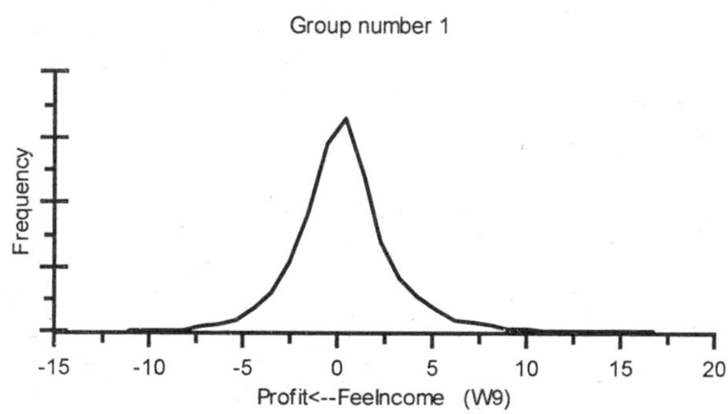

Figure 33 : Posterior Frequesncy Polygon Distribution of the Fee-Based Income and Profitability, Regression Weight (W9)

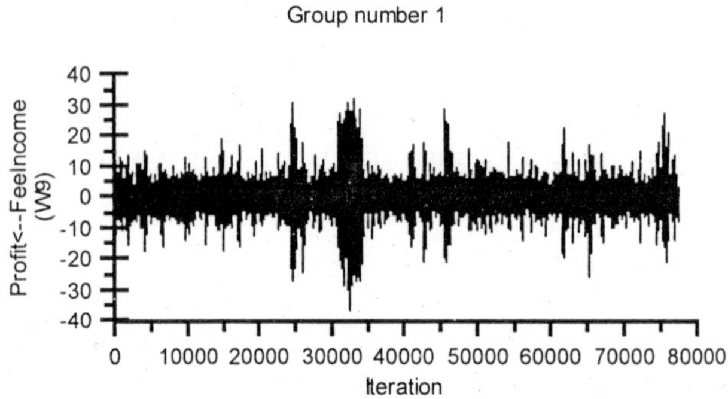

Figure 34 : Posterior Trace Plot of the ESW-NW Model for the Mediated Factor Fee-Based Income and Profitability, Regression Weight (W9)

The trace plot also called time series plot shows the sampled values of a parameter over time. This plot helps to judge how quickly the MCMC procedure converges in distribution. The following figure (Figure 34) shows the trace plot of TEM-AFC model for the mediated factor Business Income with other dimensions of business across 50,000 samples. The figure exhibits rapid up and down variation with no long-term trends or drifts. This indicates that the convergence in distribution takes place quickly.

The research model TEM-AFC, while many management scientists are most familiar with the estimation of these models using software that analyses (e.g., LISREL, AMOS), the author adopt Bayesian approach for estimation and inference in AMOS 16.0 environment. Since it offers numerous methodological and substantive advantages over alternative approaches. The table 26 shows the Bayesian convergence distribution of TEM-AFC mediated regression model. In this research, the author has adopted for the procedure of assessing convergence of MCMC (Markov Chain Monte Carlo) algorithm of maximum likelihood. To estimate the MCMC convergence, the author adopted two methods namely, convergence in distribution , convergence of posterior summaries. The values of posterior means accurately estimate the TEM-AFC mediated SEM model. From the above table the highest value of Convergence Statistics (C.S) is 1.00 which is less than the 1.002 conservative measure (Gelman et al, 2004).

Table 26
Bayesian Convergence Distribution for ESW-NW Fee-Based Income and Profitability

Mean	*S.E.*	*S.D.*	*C.S.*	*Skewness*	*Kurtosis*	*Min*	*Max*	*Name*
Regression Weights								
PROFIT<—INTINCOME	-0.126	0.006	1.432	1.000	-0.071	15.280	-17.843	22.953W1
Profit<—DivIncome	-3.616	0.042	7.195	1.000	-0.280	17.598	-103.92	89.125W2
Profit<—LeaseRent	-0.013	0.002	0.349	1.000	0.080	17.535	-4.623	5.059W3
Profit<—HPCharges	-0.066	0.002	0.382	1.000	-0.014	16.012	-4.817	4.634W4
FeeIncome<IntIncom	-0.174	0.002	0.377	1.000	0.303	20.281	-5.959	8.410W5
FeeIncome<DivIncom	0.295	0.007	1.995	1.000	0.112	19.555	-38.181	33.661W6
FeeIncome<LeaseRen	0.037	0.000	0.093	1.000	-0.412	16.630	-1.369	1.228W7
FeeIncomeHPCharges	0.047	0 000	0.098	1.000	0.123	14.805	-1.274	1.535W8
Profit<—FeeIncome	0.140	0 010	3.412	1.000	0.110	16.663	-35.637	53.915W9
Means								
INTINCOME	2126.14	1.818	536.800	1.000	0.019	1.677	-1714.4	5984.569
DivIncome	595.690	0.630	127.009	1.000	-0.007	1.725	-392.93	1501.449
LeaseRent	13473.0	10.321	2427.573	1.000	0.013	1.620	-2656.7	30481.072
HPCharges	39169.5	9.983	2760.464	1.000	0.015	2.958	8497.7	70144.578
Intercepts								
FEEINCOME	-469.427	14.762	4648.154	1.000	-0.051	15.716	-77040.	74425.000
Profit	12699.6	91.918	16800.90	1.000	0.188	17.915	234368	237291.531
Variances								
INTINCOME	2886093	13857.71	2250421.	1.000	4.792	52.157	414953	60996104.0
DivIncome	162452.	606.593	135290.7	1.000	6.537	99.541	23447.	4180642.50
LeaseRent	5830480	192695.8	46097241	1.000	4.705	44.277	663514	1005242752
HPCharges	7622511	1265567.	88966304	1.000	25.285	1089.0	841143	4841506816
e1	1268772	158713.3	2827744.	1.000	7.134	62.236	46384.	42374344.0
e2	1541638	2634192.	34395469.	1.000	5.315	36.093	284850	383830112.

REGRESSION MODEL OF THE PROFIT – ESW (NW) MEDIATED STRUCTURAL EQUATION MODEL

The path diagram for the hypothesized mediated model is given in the path diagram (see Figure 35).

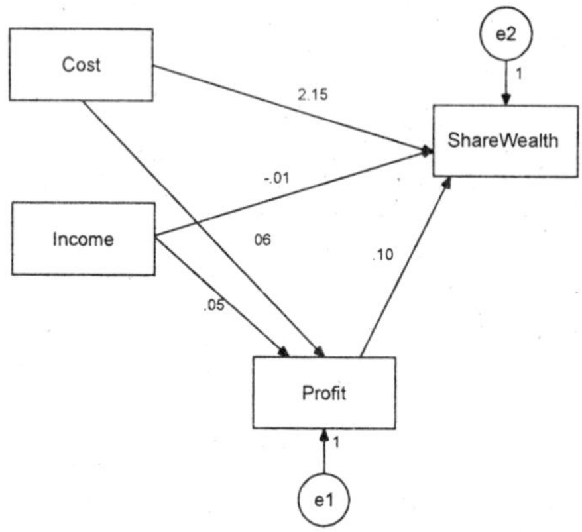

Figure 35 : ESW (NW) - PROFIT Model

The regression analysis reveals the profitability. The Income 0.05, followed by Cost 0.06. The R^2 value of 0.10 for mediating factor. The visual representation of the results suggest that the relationship between dimensions of business and mediated factor. The Income, Cost resulted observable impact on mediated factor, Profit. This model represents Asset Finance Companies may concentrate on increasing the earnings and control cost for wealth creation. The profitability is significant in creating shareholders' wealth.

Posterior Diagnostic Plots of ESW (NW) - Profit Mediated Regression Model

To check the convergence of Bayesian MCMC method the posterior diagnostic plots are analyzed. The following figure (Figures 36) shows the posterior frequency polygon of the distribution of the parameters across the 50,000 samples. The Bayesian MCMC is diagnostic plot reveals that for all the figures the normality is achieved, so the structural equation model fit is accurately estimated.

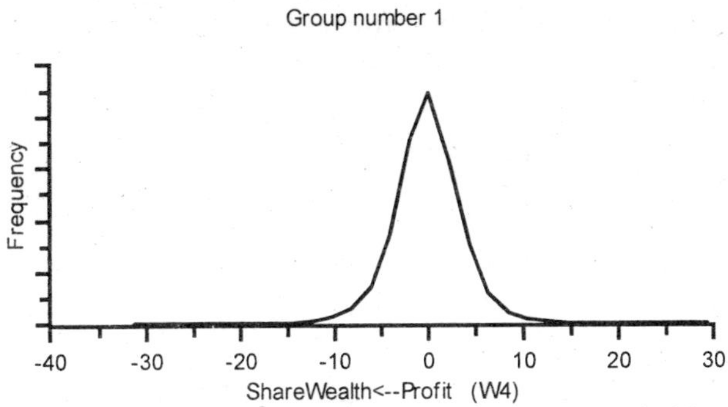

Figure 36 : Posterior Frequency Polygon of Shareholders Wealth Profit Regression Weight (W4)

To determine how long it takes for the correlation among the samples to die down, autocorrelation plot which is the estimated correlation between the sampled value at any iteration and the sampled value k iterations later for k = 1,2,3,....is analysed for ESW(NW) - PROFIT. The figure 37 shows the correlation plot of the ESW (NW) - PROFIT for the mediated factor of Business Income with other dimensions across 50,000 samples. The figures exhibits that the lag 9 and beyond, the correlation is effectively 0. This indicated that by 80 iterations, the MCMC procedure has essentially forgotten its starting position. Forgetting the starting position is equivalent to convergence in distribution. Hence, it is ensured

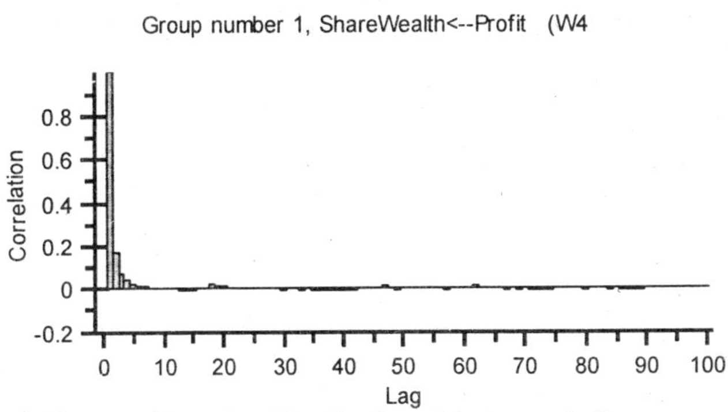

Figure 37 : Posterior Distribution of Autocorrelation among Shareholders' Wealth and Profit, Regression Weight (W4)

that convergence in distribution is attained, and that the analysis samples are indeed samples from the true posterior distribution.

The trace plot also called time series plot shows the sampled values of a parameter over time. This plot helps to judge how quickly the MCMC procedure converges in distribution. The following figure (Figure 38) shows the trace plot of ESW (NW) – PROFIT model for the mediated factor PROFIT with other dimensions of business performance across 50,000 samples. The figure exhibits rapid up and down variation with no long-term trends or drifts. This indicates that the convergence in distribution takes place quickly.

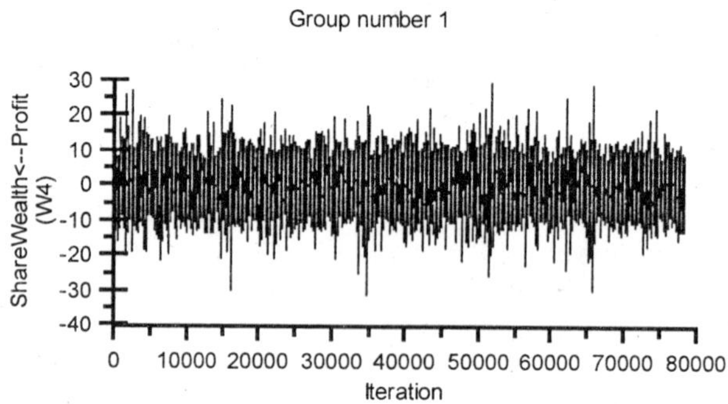

Figure 38 : Posterior Trace Plot of the ESW-NW Model for the Mediated Factor Shareholders Wealth and Profit, Regression Weight (W4)

The research model ESW (NW) - PROFIT, while many management scientists are most familiar with the estimation of these models using software that analyses (e.g., LISREL, AMOS), the author adopt Bayesian approach for estimation and inference in AMOS 16.0 environment. Since it offers numerous methodological and substantive advantages over alternative approaches. The table 27 shows the Bayesian convergence distribution of ESW (NW) - PROFIT mediated regression model. In this research, the author has adopted for the procedure of assessing convergence of MCMC (Markov Chain Monte Carlo) algorithm of maximum likelihood. To estimate the MCMC convergence, the author adopted two methods namely, convergence in distribution, convergence of

Table 27

Bayesian Convergence Distribution For ESW-NW and Profitability

	Mean	*S.E.*	*S.D.*	*C.S.*	*Skewness*	*Kurtosis*	*Min*	*Max*	*Name*
Regression Weights									
ShareWealth←Cost	2.155	0.008	0.798	1.000	-0.054	2.432	-3.884	7.648	W1
ShareWealth←Income	-0.010	0.005	0.498	1.000	0.037	2.181	-3.107	3.853	W2
Profit←Income	0.045	0.001	0.073	1.000	-0.217	3.052	-0.689	0.533	W3
ShareWealth←Profit	-0.063	0.024	3.731	1.000	-0.045	2.757	-32.600	26.334	W4
Profit←Cost	-0.062	0.001	0.117	1.000	0.166	2.449	-1.081	0.851	W5
Means									
Cost	24427.919	12.192	2900.821	1.000	-0.026	1.549	5835.942	46767.445	
Income	57227.563	23.834	4648.731	1.000	0.007	1.476	29432.795	87874.703	
Intercepts									
Profit	6710.007	26.548	3334.790	1.000	0.091	3.313	-20002.434	33069.516	I1
ShareWealth	-384.245	200.878	32542.755	1.000	0.011	2.352	-225159.641	255889.594	I2
Variances									
Cost	83155734.621	917663.953	61750566.162	1.000	3.415	19.498	10126172.00	800780032.	
Income	217672389.09	1765005.49	159818267.60	1.000	3.125	16.753	27275346.00	235569792	
e1	3568693.968	161920.841	3748048.512	1.001	3.943	21.074	325296.031	38273452.0	
e2	146401286.41	4265227.75	134184448.69	1.001	2.668	9.520	13075933.00	122611635	

posterior summaries. The values of posterior means accurately estimate the ESW (NW) - PROFIT mediated SEM model. From the above table the highest value of Convergence Statistics (C.S) is 1.00 which is less than the 1.002 conservative measure (Gelman et al, 2004). This reveals profit is the ultimate aim of the shareholders' wealth in asset finance companies operating in non-banking finance sector. Asset finance companies should concentrate on reducing administrative expenses and increase the fee income for creation of investors' wealth.

REGRESSION MODEL OF THE ESW (NW) – INCOME (DEFLATOR) MEDIATED STRUCTURAL EQUATION MODEL

The path diagram for the hypothesized mediated model is given in the path diagram (see Figure 39).

The author has taken the wholesale price index for deflating financial parameters for finding out real picture of asset finance companies in Tamil Nadu. The wholesale price index had been from Reserve Bank of India Bulletin – 2007.

The regression analysis reveals the earnings for wealth creation. The Profit 1.46, followed by Expenses 2.39. The R^2 value of 0.16 for mediating factor. The visual representation

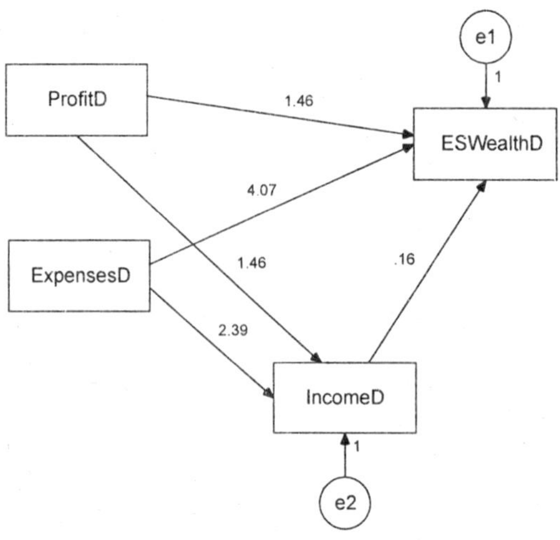

Figure 39 : ESW (NW) – Income Model (Deflator)

of the results suggest that the relationship between dimensions of business and mediated factor. The Profitability, Expenses have not resulted significant impact on mediated factor, Income. It shows the profitability and expenses have not resulted influence in Shareholders' Wealth creation This model represents Asset Finance Companies may concentrate on increasing the earnings for wealth creation. The earnings is alone significant in creating shareholders' wealth.

Posterior Diagnostic Plots of ESW (NW)–Income Mediated Regression Model

To check the convergence of Bayesian MCMC method the posterior diagnostic plots are analyzed. The following figure (Figures 40) shows the posterior frequency polygon of the distribution of the parameters across the 50,000 samples. The Bayesian MCMC is diagnostic plot reveals that for all the figures the normality is achieved, so the structural equation model fit is accurately estimated.

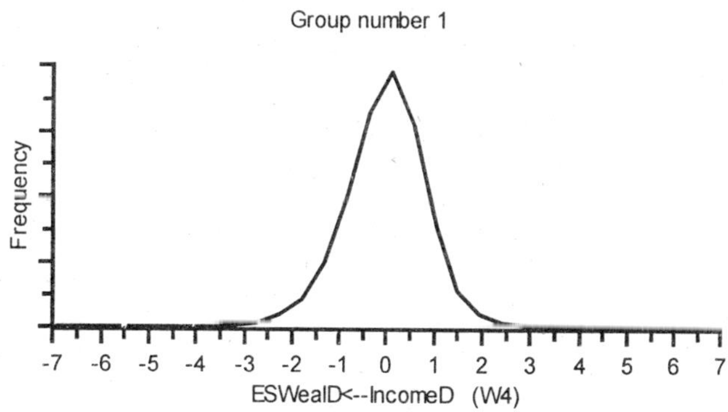

Figure 40 : Posterior Frequency Polygon of Shareholders Wealth and Income (Deflator), Regression Weight (W4)

To determine how long it takes for the correlation among the samples to die down, autocorrelation plot which is the estimated correlation between the sampled value at any iteration and the sampled value k iterations later for k = 1,2,3,....is analysed for ESW(NW) - PROFIT. The figure 41 shows the correlation plot of the ESW (NW) - PROFIT for the mediated factor of Business Income with other dimensions across 50,000 samples. The figures exhibits that the lag 45 and beyond, the correlation is effectively 0. This indicated that by 80 iterations, the MCMC procedure has essentially forgotten its starting position. Forgetting the starting position is equivalent to convergence in distribution. Hence, it is ensured that convergence in distribution is attained, and that the analysis samples are indeed samples from the true posterior distribution.

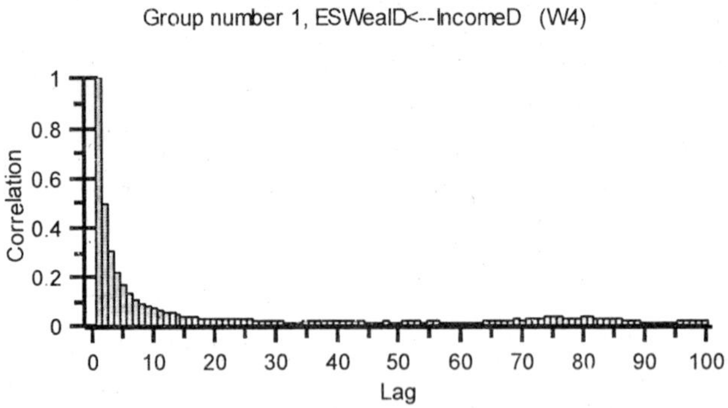

Figure 41 : Posterior Distribution of Autocorrelation among Shareholders' Wealth and Income (Deflator), Regression Weight (W4)

The trace plot also called time series plot shows the sampled values of a parameter over time. This plot helps to judge how quickly the MCMC procedure converges in distribution. The following figure (Figure 42) shows the trace plot of ESW (NW) – PROFIT model for the mediated factor PROFIT with other dimensions of business performance across 50,000 samples. The figure exhibits rapid up and down variation with no long-term trends or drifts. This indicates that the convergence in distribution takes place quickly.

The research model ESW (NW) - INCOME, while many management scientists are most familiar with the estimation of these models using software that analyses (e.g., LISREL, AMOS), the author adopt Bayesian approach for estimation and inference in AMOS 16.0 environment. Since it offers numerous methodological and substantive advantages over alternative approaches. The Table 28 shows the Bayesian

Table 28

Bayesian Convergence Distribution For ESW-NW and Income (Deflator)

	Mean	*S.E.*	*S.D.*	*C.S.*	*Skewness*	*Kurtosis*	*Min*	*Max*	*Name*
Regression Weights									
IncomeD←ProfitD	0.946	0.032	1.758	1.000	-0.629	0.745	-8.199	10.093	W1
IncomeD←ExpensesD	2.266	0.012	1.270	1.000	-0.483	2.447	-6.890	10.510	W2
ESWealD←ExpensesD	3.685	0.028	2.776	1.000	0.246	2.044	-16.418	22.371	W3
ESWealD←IncomeD	-0.045	0.009	0.906	1.000	-0.318	2.340	-6.935	6.656	W4
Means									
ProfitD	5648.851	2.764	579.458	1.000	0.052	2.199	546.241	10868.246	
ExpensesD	8282.906	5.568	767.028	1.000	0.141	3.677	1929.962	16566.617	
Intercepts									
IncomeD	17370.481	262.569	16821.933	1.000	0.725	1.540	-61208.055	130707.313	I1
ESWealD	124.652	[illegible]97.105	25846.806	1.000	-0.046	3.072	-209625.734	201448.219	I2
Variances									
ProfitD	3027789.704	59036.083	2644542.444	1.000	3.541	18.431	379442.969	33800352.000	
ExpensesD	5343437.669	261640.815	6081591.021	1.000	9.174	129.783	611007.313	118932640.000	
e2	30847659.182	1085225.064	31679431.641	1.001	2.804	10.333	1957191.125	297272416.000	
e1	75712803.132	4109419.466	33809069.896	1.001	3.637	18.804	2376837.000	921180288.000	

convergence distribution of ESW (NW) – INCOME mediated regression model. In this research, the author has adopted for the procedure of assessing convergence of MCMC (Markov

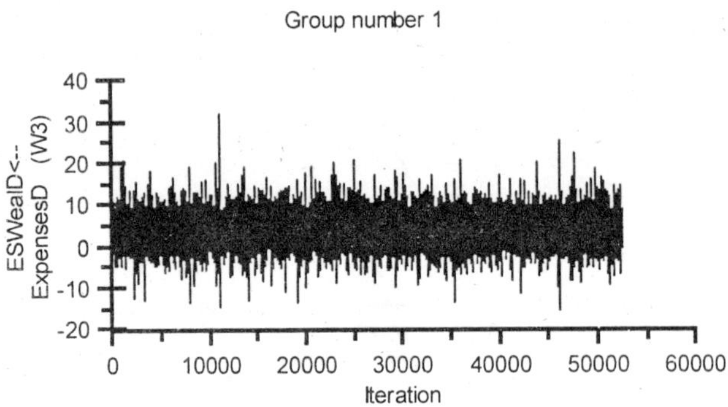

Figure 42 : Posterior Trace Plot of the ESW-NW Model for the Mediated Factor Shareholders Wealth and Income (Deflator), Regression Weight (W4)

Chain Monte Carlo) algorithm of maximum likelihood. To estimate the MCMC convergence, the author adopted two methods namely, convergence in distribution , convergence of posterior summaries. The values of posterior means accurately estimate the ESW (NW) – INCOME mediated SEM model. From the above table the highest value of Convergence Statistics (C.S) is 1.00 which is less than the 1.002 conservative measure (Gelman et al, 2004). After deflating the nominal data, the research found that income is the core source for investors for the real value. Here, this model represents for asset finance companies and investors should realize the real picture for investing their resources in different business activities through diversifications.

CONCLUSION

In this chapter, the strategic methodology adopted for performance measurement has been dwelt in detail and the foundation for this methodology; this is followed by the explanation on the population and the sample, sample companies' scale of public funds, the data collection approach and data analysis were presented in detail. Finally, the model for various performance measures were empirically tested. The empirical tests show asset finance companies should boost their earnings during economic prosperity and in recessionary periods cost control strategies would be the viable tool. However, the cost control measures should aim at reduction in administration expenses than staffing expenses. A good risk management strategy is to increase the proportion of fee-based earnings and asset based financing should be moderate.

NOTES

1. Enterprise value is the sum of net operating assets and present value of expected residual operating income where net operating asset equals the difference between operating assets (assets produced out of operations, eg. accounts receivable) and operating liabilities (obligations out of operations eg. accounts payable). Refer Penman Stephen (2001).
2. Interchangeably referred as core earnings, earnings out of principal business activities.
3. Operating Profit is the difference between the income generated out of operations and expenses incurred for conducting the operations. Refer George Foster (2002).
4. it is a financial ratio used to measure the firm's short-term liquidity scenario. It is calculated dividing the current liabilities by current assets.
5. Source: various publications of newspapers and articles in the leading magazines circulated widely in Tamil Nadu
6. Source: Trends in Banking Non Banking Finance Companies published by the Reserve Bank of India, available *online: www.rbi.org.in*
7. Net interest income is the difference between the interest income and interest expense. The interest spread is calculated on the net interest income.
8. Examples of the Comprehensive income items are unrealized gain or loss on sale of securities marked-to-market.
9. refer Reserve Bank of India circular on reclassification of non-banking finance companies (Reserve Bank 2006).

4

STRATEGIC INVESTMENT MANAGEMENT APPROACHES

INTRODUCTION

The findings obtained from the statistical test performed on the hypotheses, the structural equation mediated models *BEM–ESW (NW)*, *Profit-Cost*, *TEM-AFC*, *Profit-ESW (NW)*, and *ESW-Income (Deflator)* regression models are given in previous chapter. Based on the findings the overall performance picture are summarized for the investors, stakeholders, and executives for taking decision on investing and/or diversifying into a new business activity. Finally, the chapter will bring the scope for future research.

The analysis in the previous chapter show that the improvement in net owned funds is mainly due to substantial issue of the new shares and preferential shares. It attribute the reasons for decline in the trend are due to stock market scams affecting new issues, frequent closure of finance companies and increasing cost of public deposits due to competition from financial institutions and banks. However, the compounded annual growth is more than 8% and even surpassed the national industrial trend.

The skewness in shareholders' funds is because of increase in cost of operations, which affected the profitability profile of the companies, particularly those operating in traditional areas of business like leasing and hire purchase activities. The financing cost can be brought down, if the banks and financial institutions raise the internal accruals through more retention of earnings. It is the cheapest source of finance, not costless given the opportunity cost. But the asset finance companies in Tamil Nadu are having a formidable compounded annual growth when compared with industry performance.

Further, the enforcement of regulations on group exposure and capital market exposure norms, and shift to new tax regime have affected the internal funds position of the asset finance companies. However, the positive upward movement in recent years is due to moderation in tax liability provided scope of higher retention of earnings.

As far as the external funds are concerned, the issue of guidelines and restrictions on exposure to non-banking finance set by the banks, the term loan disbursements by the banks to finance companies have fallen more significantly in 2001. Further the closure of many finance companies and rampancy of mismanagement have forced the banks to desist from active lending except to high profile finance companies.

The enforcement of regulations on group exposure and capital market exposure norms, and shift to new tax regime have affected the internal funds position of the asset finance companies. However, the positive upward movement during 2003-04 is due to moderation in tax liability provided scope of higher retention of earnings.

The recent relaxation of norms on issue of commercial paper is helping the asset finance companies to have access to unsecured funds. The compounded annual growth revealed that the asset finance companies in the state have more access to these funds than the national players.

The stability of secured funds in the form of non-convertible debenture, banks' working capital assistance, and cash credit accommodation is attributed to restrictions on access to public deposits, high cost of funds for unsecured loans, and availability of collateralized assets for availing cash credits.

In 1997 & 1998, many of the automobile manufacturers witnessed contraction of sales and economy was also on downward trend, which led to low off take and the poor credit recovery due to asset stripping. However, the economy is on positive track since 1999 and riskiness of assets was diversified through higher volume in hire purchase activities than in leasing.

The risk aversion attitude of management, stringent provisioning norms, and statutory maintenance of liquid assets force the linear positive distribution in investment. Further, this period witness increased diversification of business in the areas of insurance, asset management, and mutual fund through new subsidiaries by high profile companies.

On whole, the asset financing in the form of hired stock holdings, and leased assets is on the decline. The reason is that the finance companies are resorting to short term financing than long-term risky financing. The asset restructuring through sale of recoverable to infuse funds into the companies is main reason for decline in short –term asset holdings.

Northward movement in cost of operations, limited access to cheaper finance, stringent risk asset provisioning have taken toll on the asset finance companies. Diversification of risk through asset restructuring, sale of assets to asset managers and exploration into new business such as insurance, healthcare, travel management have reduced holdings in leased assets as seen from negative annual compound growth.

The enforcement of strict norms on business activities, limited avenues for business development, high-risk involvement in asset financing, and reduction in exposure to capital market investments due to high incidence of manipulation in secondary market are the reasons for positive trend observed in the fee-based income generating activities. The stiff competition has forced the non-bank finance companies to change their business strategies like shift from traditional fund-based activities to fee-based activities and diversification into new businesses. The change in business strategies has, altogether, affected the earnings in core business sector (Ingres 2006).

The increased competition from commercial banks with low finance charges, declining market share, non-recoverability and asset stripping, mounting non-performing loans have forced the companies to reduce their funds-based activities. However, the low profile companies continue concentrate on funds-based activities in spite of increased competition due to their personalized customer care, good rapport with customers make it easy to enforce recovery, and their geographical proximity with customers.

With the entry of multinationals and banks in asset financing, increasing cost of funds resulting higher finance charges, enhancement of risk profile of asset leasing have seriously affected the lease business profile of asset finance companies. The downtrend is more pronounced in last phase (2001-2004). The legal impediments in enforcing the leasing covenants through recovery mechanism is affecting the leasing business.

With the competition is growing and entry of many new players, shift consumption behaviour, risk aversion of executives; uptrend in the hire purchase activities has been halted. With the hire purchase financing market is becoming more mature, high cost of operations affected the uptrend from 2000. It is observed, from early 2001, that the trend has been on steady downward movement.

With the prescription of group and capital market exposure norms on investments in subsidiaries, and net owned funds requirements, the companies sold substantial holdings in subsidiaries or in capital markets. Besides, the stock market manipulation in 2001 have seriously jeopardized the value of underlying securities. But with the economy back on track and relaxation of capital market exposure have paved way for increase in earnings from non-business activities.

The interest burden has been quite high till 1999. The reasons are higher interest paid for public deposits to attract them in the face of competition from banks, and to arrest the outflow in the wake of failure of quite a number of finance companies. The interest burden for asset finance companies has drastically increased in 1997-98 due to higher inflation coupled with heavy competition from banks.

The reasons for increase in staff cost are increase in cost of living, higher economic growth; salary increases prevalent in the sector as well as across the industries. Recently, trend in the staff related expenditure is downtrend and the cost is coming down substantially through introduction of voluntary retirement scheme, redeployment of excess staff to new business activities.

The negative trend exhibited in this statutory requirement is mainly due to previous higher provision for bad loans and strengthened recovery mechanism resulting in higher collection of receivables and bad debts. However, the downtrend is perceptible due to strengthened recovery mechanism, lower disbursements, and sound credit appraisal and post sanction follow-up.

Low inflation coupled with higher utilization of infrastructure, easy access to cheap finance during 1997 & 1999, control of other expenditures are the major reasons for the fairly skewed distribution. However, strict vigil has to be maintained on the cost side as it can adversely affect the profitability of these companies.

Core operations show positive skewness during this period. Lease disbursements are more pronounced in 1996-98 than in other period. Moreover, easier cash credit accommodation provided by the banks has aided increase in cash flow generation from operations.

The pronounced downtrend in 2000 is mainly due to high inflation, economic growth driving high cost of funds, reduced business from stiff competition from banks with huge funds on relaxation of liquidity requirements. Given this feature, an increase in the rate of inflation drives down the real rate of return not just on money, but also on assets in general. The implied reduction in real returns exacerbates credit market frictions (Boyd J 2000).

Regression Model for Bem-Esw (NW)

The standardized parameter estimates for mediated model explains the existing relationships between the mediating factor business income and shareholders' wealth. For the mediating income r=.20 is accepted. The non–business income r value =.02 is accepted for mediating factor. Non-Business expenses r =-.55 is significant to shareholder's wealth. NBI and BE are not significant to shareholders' wealth. NBE and BE is not significant to mediating factor.

Regression Model for Cost - Profit

The standardized parameter estimates for mediated model explains the existing relationships between the mediating factor Administrative Expenses and Profit. For the mediating Administrative Expenses r =.50 is accepted. Loan Interest r = -.08, Finance Charges r = -.21, Staff Salary r = 0.48, Provisions r = -.08 are significant for fee income as mediating factor. Loan Interest r =.23, Finance Charges r = -.06, Staff Salary r = 0.13, Provisions r = -.30 are significant for profit. Above stated factors established there exist linear relationship with profit and cost.

Regression Model for TEM-AFC

The standardized parameter estimates for mediated model explains the existing relationships between the mediating factor Fee Income and Profit. For the mediating fee income r...17 is accepted. Interest income r = -.17, Dividend Income r = .29, Lease Rent r = .04 and HP Charges r = .05 are significant for fee income as mediating factor for profitability. Interest income r = -.12, Lease Rent r = -.02 and HP Charges r = -.07 are significant for profit. Dividend Income r = -3.61 for the profit is not accepted.

Regression Model for Overall Performance (Shareholders' Wealth)

The standardized parameter estimates for mediated model explains the existing relationships between the mediating factor profit and other business dimensions. For the mediating the profit r =.10, income r = -0.01 is accepted. The cost and income is not significant in shareholders' wealth. The cost and income dimension are accepted for mediating factor, profit.

Regression Model for Overall Performance (Shareholders' Wealth) - Deflator

The figure 4.38 standardized parameter estimates for mediated model explains the existing relationships between the mediating factor income and shareholders' wealth. For the mediating income r =.16 is accepted. The profit and expenses are not significant in shareholders' wealth. The profit and expenses dimension are not accepted for mediating factor, income.

Structural Equation Regression Model for Overall Performance (Shareholders' Wealth)

The conceptual model empirically proved by AMOS graphic environment. Cost, Income and Profit are very essential for creating the shareholders' wealth in asset finance companies in India. Strategic cost control will influence the profitability in asset finance companies. If asset finance companies would follow above empirical model, which leads to sustainability of their business. If there is uncontrollable risk in their business, new entrepreneur who like to start a business in asset finance sector, may follow above ESW (NW) –AFC mediated model. This model paves the way for strategic management in profitability of asset finance companies operating in non-banking financial sector in India.

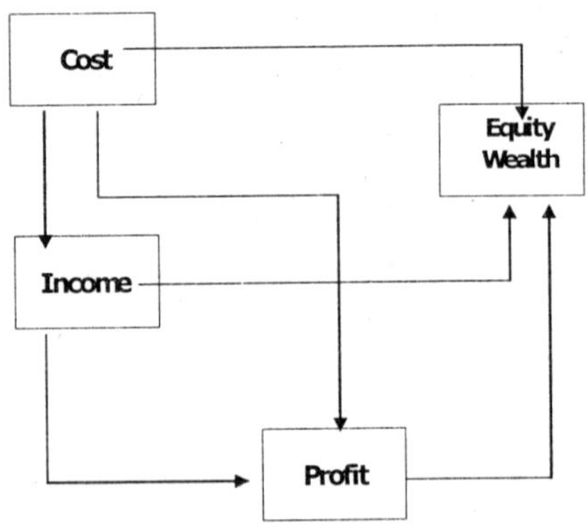

Figure 1 : ESW (NW) – AFC Mediated Model

The conceptual mediated model (deflator) is empirically examined through AMOS Graphic environment. This model will help the shareholders for investing their resources with diversification of business. The essence of deflator model reveals the real picture of monetary value in the macroeconomic environment. This model will help the promoters of asset finance companies through investigate the economic indicators, general price level and rate of interest for diversification of their business for creation of shareholders' wealth. The above findings of the research will ensure normality of the business of the asset finance companies. It is a new approach for applying the strategic management for sustainability of asset finance companies in India. This research reveals another key finding to control the administrative expenses for creation of wealth and asset finance companies would concentrate more on fee-based activities for their sustainability. The author concludes that a strategic approach for diversification of business on fee-based activities is to protect the interests of the shareholders.

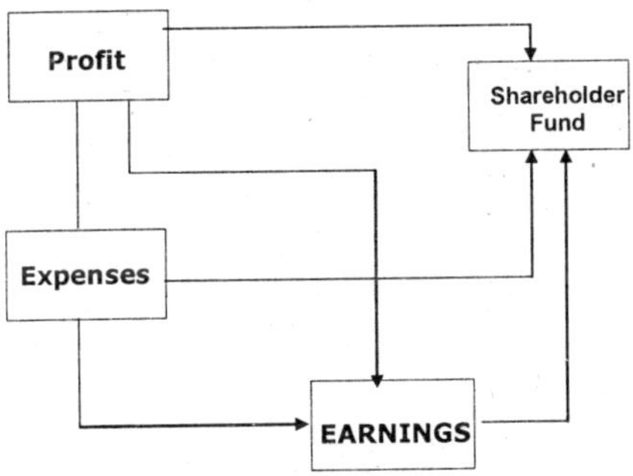

Figure 2 : ESW –AFC Mediated Model - Deflator

INVESTMENT STRATEGIES FOR THE NEW ENTREPREURS

Presently, the asset finance companies are facing competition from commercial banks and major players in financial services like *ICICI, HDFC* from the private sector and multinational financial services conglomerates like *CITIBANK (CITIGROUP), HSBC Financial Services*. Therefore, it is imperative that the asset finance companies should reorient their business strategies to withstand the competition, economic conditions, and to emerge successful leader.

The asset finance companies should not stay away completely from the leasing and hire purchase activities. As the Indian economy is growing at a faster pace, the shifts in consumption patterns are so dynamic. The attitude of common treatment automobiles such as Motor Cars, Motorcycles as luxury is changing. The possession of these, are felt, as necessaries. Asset finance companies should focus more on consumer automobile financing than on truck financing, which is quite risky. There is a felt need for the asset finance companies to expand their geographical reach as the commercial banks are expanding their geographical spread.

The asset finance companies should realize the need for consolidating their businesses. These companies are promoted by the local wealthy people either as private limited or public limited company. Their continued desire to stick to individual corporate identity could endanger their very existence. They shall go in for mergers with group companies and function as a division within it or acquire the business of the promoter business. They should realize that mergers and acquisitions could alone make them strong, dynamic and vibrant. Any delay in consolidation could prove to be disastrous.

The asset finance companies, operating throughout the state, should enter into allied financial services like insurance, money transfer, and micro-finance as agents or facilitators to the commercial banks and insurance companies. They should explore the opportunities thrown open by deregulation of entry into insurance sector, as a consortium to start with. They should concentrate more on fee-based activities like money transfer agency, travel and tourism services, healthcare facilitator.

They can also explore the new funds-based business like travel financing, healthcare financing, education financing, and micro-finance. The funds-based activities carry, though, high risk are remunerative in terms of their personalized customer care, local reach. Funds-based financing for activities like infrastructure financing, festival financing are quite risk free businesses. Asset finance companies, operating locally, shall form a consortium to finance big yet returns oriented projects.

The asset finance companies with high level of public deposits should not deploy their funds in bonds than required by law. It is observed that the reason for parking funds in such portfolios is mainly downtrend in automobile financing, leasing activities. They should realize that public deposits are high cost funds. Therefore, the need to deploy them in efficiently in asset financing is very demanding.

The advantages of asset finance companies are their personal rapport with their customers. They shall utilize this opportunity to promote fee-based services to them. Prior knowledge on borrowers is very much a requirement. They shall become users of credit information bureau. In the case of small companies, they shall jointly create a database on creditworthiness of customers.

The asset finance companies should concentrate on reducing the administrative expenditures through utilizing the available infrastructure efficiently than to have a desire to cut the staff size. It is recommended that small asset finance companies should concentrate more on their core business than to diversify their operations. In case of small companies, the profit per staff is lower than their high profile counter parts. Recovery mechanism should be strengthened to interact with the borrowers frequently than to resort to legal proceedings.

CONCLUSION

In terms of future research, business profile of the competitors like banks, large financial institutions can be analysed to identify the strength and weaknesses of the asset finance companies vis-à-vis its competitors. There is a scope for micro-level performance study of the asset finance companies. Such micro level study can bring the key strategies that are required for the development of non-banking financial sector. The customer satisfaction or service quality can be studied to identify the customer needs for services and the utility value of the services offered by the asset finance companies. A comparative study of financial services across the countries can throw more light on divergence in business strategies and suggest formulation of key business strategies in tune with the global conditions.

REFERENCES

Acemoglu, Daron, and Simon Johnson, (2005), "Unbundling Institutions," Journal of Political Economy, 113 (5), pp.949-995.

Ahluwalia, M. S. (2002), "Economic Reforms in India since 1991: Has Gradualism Worked?" *Journal of Economic Perspectives*, 16, (3), pp.67-88.

Ahluwalia Montek S. (2002), Financial Sector Reform in India, paper presented at conference on Financial Sector Reform Across Asia: Facts, Analyses, Solutions, John F. Kennedy School of Government, Harvard University, December.

Altman et.al, Haldeman G Robert & Narayanan. P (1977), "Zeta Analysis: A New m Model to Identify Bankruptcy Risk of Corporations", *Journal of Banking and Finance*, Spring.

Altman Edward E, Saunders Anthony (2000), "An Analysis and Critique of the BIS Proposal on Capital Adequacy and Ratings", paper presented in Symposium, Stern Business School, NYU Salomon Center, February 25th, 2000, pp.3-23

Ananth Bindu, Barooah Bastavee, Rushismita Rupalee, Bhatnagar Aparna (2004), "A Blueprint for the delivery of Comprehensive Financial Services to the Poor in India", Centre for Micro Finance, Working Paper Series, November, pp. 3-32.

Ang J., Peterson P.P., (1984), "The Leasing Puzzle", *Journal of Finance*, 1984, pp. 1055-1065.

Aragon, G A (1989), "Financial Management", Allyn and Bacon, Massachusetts.

Arbuckle, J.L, Wothke W, (2006), "AMOS 7.0 Users' Guide", Chicago, Small Waters Corporation.

Athey M.J, Majumdar S.K (1994), "Internal Funds and Corporate Investment in India", Industrial and Corporate Change", 7 (1), pp.109-152.

Ball Ray, Watts Ross, (2002), "Some Time Series Properties of Accounting Income", *The Journal of Finance* (2003), pp. 663-681.

Bansal L.K, (1994), "Leasing Environment in India", *Finance India,* Vol. VIII, No. 5, September, pp. 417-422.

Bacidore Jeffrey M, Boquist John A, Milbourn Todd T., Thakor Anjan V. (1997), "The Search for the Best Financial Performance Measure", *Financial Analysts Journal,* May/June, pp. 11-20.

Barth R James, Gerard Capario, Jr, Levine Ross, (2001), "Financial Regulation and Performance Cross-Country Evidence", Working Papers–Central Bank of Chile, No 118, November, pp 1-29.

Barth J. R., Capario G., Levine R., (2001a), "Banking Systems around the Globe: Do Regulations and Ownership affect Performance and Stability?", Prudential Supervision What work and What doesn't, Editor: Mishkin F.S, University of Chicago Press, April. Full.

Barth J R, Capario G, Levine R, (2001b), "Commercial Banking Structure, Regulation and Performance: An International Comparison", Economics Working Papers 97-6, Washington, Office of the Comptroller of Currency, U.S.Treasury, March. Full

Basle Committee on Banking Supervision,(1999), "Credit Risk Modeling: Current Practices and Applications," Basle, April.

Basle Committee on Banking Supervision,(1999), "A New Capital Adequacy Framework", Basle, June 1999.

Batisa-Foguet J.M, Coenders G, (2000), "Modelos de Ecuaciones Estructurales (Structural Equation Models)", Madrid, Spain, La Muralla

Behn, B., Riley, R. (1999), "Using Nonûnancial Information to Predict Financial Performance: The Case of the US Airline Industry", *Journal of Accounting, Auditing, and Finance*, 29–56.

Besley T., Levenson A.L.,(1996), "The Role of Informal Finance in Household Capital Accumulation: Evidence from Taiwan", *The Economic Journal,*Vol. 106, No. 434, January, pp. 39-59.

Benston George.J, (1995), "Branch Banking and Economies of Scale", The *Journal of Finance* Vol. XX, No. 2, May, pp. 312-330.

Berger N Allen, Humphrey B David, (1997), "Efficiency of Financial Institutions: International Survey and Directions for Future Research", Financial Institutions Center, Wharton School, University of Pennsylvania, 97-05, pp. 1-51.

Berger, A.N., and L.J. Mester (2001), "Explaining the Dramatic Changes in Performance of U.S. Banks: Technological Change, Deregulation, and Dynamic Changes in Competition." Working Paper, University of Pennsylvania. June, Full.

Berlin Mitchell, Mester J Loretta, (1997), "On the Profitability and Cost of Relationship Lending", Financial Institutions Center, Wharton School, University of Pennsylvania, July, 97-43, pp. 3-32.

Berk B Jonathan, (1997), "Does Size Really Matter?", *Financial Analysts Journal*, Sep./Oct., pp 12-18.

Beuselinck Christof, (2000), "The Economic Impact of Leasing", Universiteit Gent Working Papers, *Faculty of Economics and Business Administration*, April, pp 1-23.

Bevan, A.A. and Danbolt, J. (2000), "Dynamics in the Determinants of Capital Structure in the UK". Working Paper 9/2000, University of Glasgow, Full.

Bhattacharya.H, (2004), "How to Read a Balance Sheet–Adapted to Indian Laws and Requirements", Oxford & IBH Publishing Co 17th Reprint, pp, 3-162.

Bhattacharyya, A., A. Bhattacharyya, and S.C. Kumbhakar (1997), "Changes in Economic Regime and Productivity Growth: A Study of Indian Public Sector Banks." *Journal of Comparative Economics* 25, pp. 196–219.

Bhattacharyya, A., Lovell, C.A. Knox, and P. Sahay (1997), "The Impact of Liberalization on the Productive Efficiency of Indian Commercial Banks." *European Journal of Operational Research*, 21, pp. 332–345.

Bhoi. B.K, (2000), "Mergers and Acquisitions: An Indian Experience", Reserve Bank Occasional Papers, Vol. 21, No. 1, Summer, pp. 133-166.

Black, A., Wright, J., Bachman, J., Makall, M., Wright, P. (1998), "In Search of Shareholder Value: Managing the Drivers of Performance", Pitman Pubn

Black, A., Wright, J., Bachman, J., Makall, M., Wright, P. (1998), "In search of Shareholder Value: Managing the Drivers of Performance", Pitman Pub.

Boyd B. (1991), "Strategic Planning and Financial Performance: A Meta-analytical Review", *Journal of Management Studies*, 28.

Boyd H.John, Levine Ross, Smith D. Bruce, (2000), "The Impact of Inflation on Financial Sector Performance", World Bank, Working Paper, February, pp. 2-33.

Brahmankar S.D, Shukla R. K., (2003), "Consumer Finance for White Goods: Cause for Cautious Optimism", *Margin,* Vol. 35, No. 2, Sep, pp. 19-33.

Brandt Nicola, (2004), "Business Dynamics, Regulation and Performance", OECD Science, Technology and Industry Working Papers, STI Working Papers 2004/3, pp. 3-32.

Brigham E Eugene, Ehrhardt C Michael, (2004), "Financial Management – Theory and Practice", Thomson (South-Western) Asia Pts Ltd, First Reprint, pp. 74-99, 784-800, 835-904.

Broome O Whitfield, (2004), "Statement of Cash Flows: Time for Change!" *Financial Analysts Journal,* March/April, pp 16-22.

Brownbridge.M, Kirkpatrick.C, (2000), "Financial Regulation in Developing Countries", *Journal of Development Studies,* October, Vol. 37, No. 1, pp 1-24.

Bruce, R., McKern, B., Pollard, I. and Skully, M. (1991), "Handbook of Australian Corporate Finance", 4th edn, Butterworths, Sydney.

Byrnes, P. (1985), "The Effect of Ownership on Efficiency: A Nonparametric Programming Approach," PhD Dissertation, Southern Illinois University, Carbondale, Illinois.

CARE (2006), "Industry Comments–Non-Banking Finance Companies", Credit Analysis & Reseach Ltd, available *online: www.careratings.com.*

Cebenoyan Sinan (2001), " Risk Management, Capital Structure and Lending at Banks", October, available *online: www.ssrn.org/papers.htm*

Chanda Rupa, (2005), "Trade in Financial Services: India's Opportunities and Constraints", Working Paper, Indian Council for Research on International Economic Relations, January, No. 152, pp 1-115.

Chaudhuri, Saumitra (2002), "Some Issues of Growth and Profitability in Indian Public Sector Banks", *Economic and Political Weekly,* June.

Christopher Woodruff, (1999), Interfirm Relationships and Informal Credit in Vietnam," *Quarterly Journal of Economics,* 114, pp. 1285-1320.

Cihak Martin, Podpiera Richard (2005), "Bank Behaviour in Developing Countries: Evidence from East Africa", IMF Working Paper, WP.05/129, June, pp.3-23.

Claessens, Stijn, Simeon Djankov, and Larry Lang,(2000), "The Separation of Ownership and Control in East Asian Corporations," *Journal of Financial Economics*, 58, pp. 81-112.

Collins, W., Davie, E., and Weetman, P. (1996), "Lobbying on Accounting Issues: preparer/user imbalance in the case of the operating and Financial Review". Accounting, *Auditing and Accountability Journal*, 9(1), Spring: pp. 59-76.

Colombo, E., (2001), "Determinants of Corporate Capital Structure: Evidence from Hungarian Firms," *Applied Economics*, 33, pp1689-1701.

Congdon, P. (2003), "Applied Bayesian Modelling", John Wiley & Sons.

Corder Matthew, (2004), "Assessing Risks from UK Non-bank Financial Sectors", Financial Stability Review, December, pp. 119-126.

Crisil (2006), "Rating Criteria for the Finance Companies", Crisil Ratings (Finance Sector), *available online: www.cricil.com*

Crutchley Claire E., Hudson Carl D., and Jensen Marlin R.H.(1998), "Shareholder Wealth Effects of CalPERS' Activism", *Financial Services Review*, 7(1), pp.1-10.

Dambolena G Ismael, Khourv J Sarkis, (1980), "Ratio Stability and Corporate Failure", *The Journal of Finance*, Vol. XXXV, No. 4, pp. 1017-1025.

Dangl Thomas, Zechner Josef, (2003), "Credit Risk and Dynamic Capital Structure Choice", *Journal of Financial Intermediation*, 11 (2004), pp 183-204.

David A. Cartera, James E. McNultyb, and James A. Verbruggec, (2002), "Do Small Banks Have an Advantage in Lending? An Examination of Risk-Adjusted Yields on Small Business Lending at Large and Small Banks", available online:

Davidson P, (1986), "Finance, Funding, Saving, and Investment", Journal of Post Keynesian Economics, Fall, vol. IX. No. 1, pp.101-110.

De Lucia, R D, Dixon, R H, Ferris, D T, Peters, J, and Plummer, B R (1987), "Commercial Bank Management: Functions and Objectives", Serendip Publications, Wamberal.

Demsetz Harold, Villalonga Belen (2001), "Ownership Structure and Corporate Performance", *Journal of Finance* 7, pp. 209-233.

Demsetz, Rebecca S., and Philip E. Strahan, (1997), "Diversification, Size, and Risk at Bank Holding Companies," *Journal of Money, Credit, and Banking*, 29, 300-313.

Deolalkar G.H, (1999), " The Indian Banking Sector on the Road to Progress", A Study of Financial Markets- Rising to the Challenge, available online, pp. 60-110.

DeYoung Robert, (1997), "Measuring Bank Cost Efficiency: Don't Count on Accounting Ratios", Financial Practice and Education, Spring/Summer, pp 20-31.

Dhulla, S (2001), "Consumer Durables: A Bruising Battle!", Consumer Durable Dealers Survey Report, *Indiainfoline.com*, January.

Djankov, Simeon, Rafael La Porta, Florencio Lopez-de-Silanes, and Andrei Shleifer, (2002), "The Regulation of Entry," *Quarterly Journal of Economics*, 117 (1), pp. 1-37.

D'souza, E., (2002), "Prudential Regulation in Indian Banking." *Economic and Political Weekly*, 35, 287-98

Drury, C. and Braund, S. (1990), "The Leasing Decision: a Comparison of Theory and Practice", Accounting and Business Research, 20(79), Summer: pp.179-191.

Duca John and Mary McLaughlin (1990), "Developments affecting the Profitability of Commercial Banks". Federal Reserve Bulletin, July.

Eeckhout Jan, Munshi Kaivan, (2003), "Institutional Change in the Non-Market Economy: Endogenous Matching in Chennai's Chit Fund Auctions", Working Paper, Bureau for Research in Economic Analysis of Development, June, No.33, pp 1-37.

Finnerty, J.E., Fitzsimmons, R.N. and Oliver, T.W. (1980), "Lease Capitalization and Systematic Risk", *Accounting Review*, 55(4), October: pp. 631-639.

Fixler, Dennis J., and Zieschang, Kimberly D. (1999), "The Productivity of the Banking Sector: Integrating Financial and Production Approaches to Measuring Financial Service Output," *Canadian Journal of Economics*, 32 (April), pp. 547-69.

Francis, G (2003), "Multiple Regression: Swinburne University Press.

Fraser, D. R. and Fraser, L. M. (1990), "Evaluating Commercial Bank Performance: A Guide to Financial Analysis", Bankers Publishing Co., Rolling Meadows, Illinois.

Gelman,A, Carlin J.B, Stern H.S, and Rubin D.B (2004), "Bayesian Data Analysis", 2nd ed, Boca Raton: Chapman and Hall/CRC

George Foster, (2002), "Financial Statement Analysis", Pearson Education Asia, Second Edition-Indian Reprint, pp 60-591.

Ghazouani Kamel (2006), "Cost of Capital and Investment Dynamic Behaviour of the Tunisian Non-Financial Companies", *Finance India,* Vol XX, No.4, December, pp.1365-1388.

Goodacre, A. (2001), "The Potential Impact of Enforced Lease Capitalisation in the UK retail sector", Proceedings of the Conference on Financial Reporting and Business Communication, Cardiff University, 5-6 July.

Goswami Ramadev, Venkatesh S (1999), "Understanding and Use of Credit Rating in India: A survey of individual and institutional investors", *The Journal of Applied Finance, Institute of Chartered Financial Analysts of India,* July, Vol. 5, No. 2, pp. 39-63.

Goyal Ashima, (1997), "Financial Reforms: Why Interest Rates must be kept Low", *International Journal of Development Banking,* July, Vol. 15, No. 2, pp. 15-25.

Graham, J.R. and Harvey, C.R. (2001), "The Theory and Practice of Corporate Finance: Evidence from the Field", *Journal of Financial Economics,* 60(2-3), May: 187-243.

Greenbaum Stuart I, Ali Mukthar M, Merris Randall C (1976), "Monetary Policy and Banking Profits", *The Journal of Finance,* Vol.XXXL, No.1, March, pp. 89-101.

Grifell-Tatje, E., and C.A.K. Lovell (1996), "Deregulation and Productivity Decline: The Case of Spanish Savings Banks." *European Economic Review,* 40, pp.1281–1303.

Gebhardt Günther (2001), "Announcement Effects of Financing Decisions by German Companies: Synthesis of an Empirical Research Programme", special research programmes "Empirical Capital Markets Research", Johann Wolfgang Goethe-Universität Frankfurt am Main.

Gujarati Damodar N(2004), "Basic Econometrics", Fourth Edn, Tata McGraw Hill, New Delhi.

Gup, B E, Fraser, D R, and Kolari, J W (1989): "Commercial Bank Management", John Wiley and Sons, New York.

Gupta Akash, Agarwal Rahul, (2003), "Consumer Financing Business India", *available online: www.econwpa.wustl.edu,* pp 2-13.

Gupta,L.C (1983), "Financial Ratios for Monitoring Corporate Sickness–Towards a more Systematic Approach", Oxford Univeristy Press.

Gupta U Megha, (2007), "Capital Market Focused NBFCs Demonstrate High Profitability: Strong Risk Management, a Key Contributor", Insight CRISIL RatingScan, Feb., pp 18-22.

Guruswamy S., (1998), "NBFCs–The Rating Blues", Charterd Secretary, August , pp. A169-A173.

Harihar T.S, (1998), "Non-Banking Finance Companies, The Imminent Squeeze", Chartered Financial Analyst, February, pp. 40-47.

Harker T Patrick, Zenios A Stavros, (1998), "What Drives the Performance of Financial Institutions?", Financial Institutions Center, Wharton School, University of Pennsylvania, June 98-21, pp. 1-27.

Hartman, T. and Storbeck, J. (1995), "Measuring Managerial and Program Efficiencies in a Swedish Savings and Loan," in Competing in the Global Marketplace: A Decision Science Viewpoint, eds. D. Olsen and K. Sliwa, Third International Conference Proceedings, Decision Sciences Institute, Puebla, Mexico, pp. 201–203.

Harihar T.S.(1998), "Non-Banking Finance Companies, The Imminent Squeeze", Chartered Financial Analyst, February 1998, p. 40-47.

Hempel, H G and Yawitz, J B (1977), "Financial Management of Financial Institutions", Prentice-Hall Inc., Englewood Cliffs, New Jersey.

Hochraich Diana (2006), "Indian Reforms in the Manufacturing and Financial Sectors: Winners and losers", Conference Proceedings, International Conference: The Indian Economy in the Era of Financial Globalization", September 2006, Paris, pp. 1-9.

Hodrick, R., (1992), "Dividend Yields and Expected Stock Returns: Alternative Procedures for Inference and Measurement", *Review of Financial Studies*, 5, pp. 357–386.

Holmbeck, G.N (1997), "Toward Terminological, Conceptual, and Statistical Clarity in the Study of Mediators and Moderators: Examples from the Child-clinical and Pediatric Psychology Literatures", *Journal of Consulting and Clinical Psychology*, 4, pp. 599-610.

Holmer L.W, Zenios S.A., (1995), "The Productivity of Financial Intermediation and the Technology of Financial Product Management", Operations Research, 43(6), pp. 970-982.

Huh Chan, Kim Bae Sun, (1994), "Financial Regulation and Banking Sector Performance: A Comparison of Bad Loan Problems in Japan and Korea", Economic Review, Federal Reserve Bank of San Francisco, Number 2, pp. 19-29.

Hyung–Gon Ro (2000), "Banking Industry Consolidation in Korea", BIS Paper. 4, pp.93-101.

Ingres, (2006), "Indian Non-Banking Finance Companies – Industry Comments", Ingres, *available online: www.icra.in.* pp 4-25.

Ittner D Christopher, Larcker F David, Randall Taylor (2003), "Performance Implications of Strategic Performance Measurement in Financial Services Firms", Accounting Organizations and Society, Vol 28, pp 715-741.

Ittner, C., Larcker, D. (1997), "Are Non-ûnancial Measures Leading Indicators of ûnancial Performance? An Analysis of Customer Satisfaction." , *Journal of Accounting Research,* 1–35

Jain, J. L. (1996), Strategic Planning for Asset Liability Management. *The Journal of the Indian Institute of Bankers,* 67(4).

Jeon Nam Bang (1997), "Cross-Ownership, Business Scope and Price Regulation for Financial Institutions in Industrial Countries: Implications for Financial Reforms in Korea", *International Journal of Development Banking,* Vol. 15, No. 2, July, pp. 27-30.

Jimenez Gabriel, Saurina Jesus (2004), "Collateral, Type of Lender and Relationship Banking as Determinants of Credit Risk", *Journal of Banking & Finance,* No. 28, pp. 2191-2212.

Kalish III Lionel, Gilbert Alton R, (2002), "The Influence of Bank Regulation on the Operating Efficiency of Commercial Banks", *The Journal of Finance,* pp. 1287-1298.

Kantawala.S Amita (2004), "Financial Performance of Non-Banking Finance Companies in India", *available online: http: // www.indian economics.org/material/j-s-01-9.pdf*

Kerlinger F.N, Lee H.B (2000), "Foundations of Behavioral Research", Fourth Edn, New York, Harcourt Publishers.

Khan. M.Y, (2002), "Banking Regulations and Islamic Banks in India: Status and Issues", *International Journal of Islamic Financial Services,* Vol. 2, No. 4, pp. 243-249.

Khan, M.Y, (2003), "Financial Services", Tata McGraw-Hill Publishing Company Ltd., Second Edition, pp. 1.3-5.23.

Khan Tariquallah, (1996), "Practices and Performance of Moradabad Companies: A Case Study of Pakistan's Experience", Research Paper 7, 1416H 1st Edn, Islamic Research and Training Institute, Islamic Development Bank, Jeddah, pp.13-145.

Khanna, Tarun, and Krishna Palepu (2000), "Is Group Affiliation Profitable in Emerging Markets? An Analysis of Diversified Indian Business Groups," *Journal of Finance*, 55, pp. 867-891.

King, R. and R. Levine, (1993), "Finance, Entrepreneurship and Growth: Theory and Evidence", *Journal of Monetary Economics*, 32, pp. 513-542.

Klumpes J M Paul, (2004), "Performance Benchmarking in Financial Services: Evidence from the UK Life Insurance Industry", *Journal of Business*, Vol. 77, No. 2, pp. 257-273.

Klumpes J.M. Paul (2004), "Performance Benchmarking in Financial Services: Evidence from the UK Life Insurance Industry", *Journal of Business*, Vol. 77, No. 2, pt. 1, pp. 257-273.

Koeva Petya, (2003), "The Performance of Indian Banks during Financial Liberalization", IMF working paper, June, 03/150, pp 3-32.

Kono, M., Low P., Luanga, M., Mattoo, A., Oshikawa, M., Schuknecht, L., (1997), Opening Markets in Financial Services and the Role of GATS, WTO Special Studies, World Trade Organisation, September.

Kooken, J F (1989), 'Understanding Profit Dynamics', *Bank Administration*, Vol. 65, No .7, July, pp. 14-17.

Kshirsagar S.D, (2003), "Financial Services in India: A New Perspective", *Management Review*, IIMB, June, pp 37-44.

Lev, B., (1989), "On the Usefulness of Earnings: Lessons and Directions from Two Decades of Empirical Research", *Supplement of Journal of Accounting Research*, 27, 153-192

Lawrence Peter, Longjam Ibotombi, (2003), " Financial Liberalization in India: Measuring Relative Progress", Keele Economics Research Papers, 08-December, pp. 1-25.

Lewellen G Wilbur, Long S Michael, McConnell J John, (1926), "Asset Leasing in Competitive Capital Markets", *The Journal of Finance, June*, Vol. XXXL. No. 3, pp. 787-797.

Lewellen Jonathan (2002), "Predicting Returns with Financial Ratios", *Journal of Financial Economics,* 74 (2004), pp. 209–235

Linda Allen , Sinan Cebenoyan (1991), "Bank Acquisitions and Ownership Structure: Theory and Evidence", *Journal of Banking and Finance,* 15, pp. 42-48.

Lo, Andrew Wen Chuan,(1984), Essays in Financial & Quantitative Economics, Harvard University, pp133.

Matto, Aditya, (1998), "Financial Services and the WTO: Liberalization in the Developing and Transition Economies", Staff Working Papers, World Trade Organisation, Trade in Services Division, March (TISD9803.WPF).

Mayer-Sommer, A.P. (1979), "Understanding and Acceptance of the Efficient Markets Hypothesis and its Accounting Implications", Accounting Review, 54(1), January: pp. 88-106.

Mehra Rajnish (2001), "Current Estimates and Prospects for Change", Equity Risk Premium Forum, AIMR, University of California, pp.69-66.

Merton R.C (1990), ."The Financial System and Economic Performance", *Journal of Financial Services Research,* pp. 263-300.

Merton C Robert, (1995), " Financial Innovation and the Management and Regulation of Financial Institutions", *Journal of Banking & Finance,* Vol. 39, pp. 461-481.

Mikolich Don (2004), "Economic Indicators: Where to Look", CIBC World Markets, Foreign Exchange & Money Market Sales, Second Edition.

Mohan Rakesh, (2004), "Financial Sector Reforms in India: Policies and Performance Analysis", Reserve Bank of India Bulletin, October, pp. 851-877.

Mohan, R. T. (2002), "Deregulation and Performance of Public Sector Banks." *Economic and Political Weekly,* 37, 393-95.

Mohanty Jaya, Hansda K Sanjay, Jain Rajeev, (2003), "Turnover Index of Financial Services–A Monthly Construct for India", Money & Finance, ICRA Bulletin, April-Sept, pp. 47-61.

Moore David, (2000), "Financial Services for Everyone", *The Mckinsey Quarterly,* No.1, Mckinsey Publications.

Mulye Vishaka, Sharma Ajay, Sabnavis Madan, (2002), "Valuation of NPLs", Working paper series, ICICIResearchcentre.org, March, pp. 7-36.

Myers, Stewart C. (1977), "Determinants of Corporate Borrowing." *Journal of Financial Economics*, 5, November, pp.147-75.

Nair, Tara S (2001), "Institutionalising Micro finance in India - An Overview of Strategic Issues", *Economic and Political Weekly*, 36(4), June 27, pp. 399-404.

Nair, Tara S (1998), "Meeting the Micro Credit Needs of the Poor: Issues in Focus", *The Indian Journal of Labour Economics*, July-September.

Narashimam, M (1991), "Committee on Banking Sector Reforms", Government of India, 1992.

Narashimhan C.R.L, (2004), "The Non-banking Sector from a Regulatory Prism", Article, *The Hindu*, Dec. 20th, pp. 18.

Narashimhan C.R.L, (2006), "Fine-tuning Regulatory Framework for NBFCs", Article, *The Hindu*, Dec. 1st, pp. 20.

Nissanke M.K., (2001), "Financing Enterprise Development in Sub-Saharan Africa", *Cambridge Journal of Economics*, 25, pp. 343-367.

Nisture Rege Rupa, (2003): "Theory and Experience in Financial Liberalization: Lessons for India", *available online: www.iciciresearch.org.*

Marc Orlitzky (2003), "Corporate Social and Financial Performance: A Meta-Analysis", *Organisation Studies*, Vol. 24, No. 3, pp. 403-441.

O'Sullivan E., Rassel G.R, (1999), "Research Methods for Public Administrators", New York, NY, Longman.

Oxelheim Lars, (2003), "Macroeconomic Variables and Corporate Performance", *Financial Analysts Journal*, pp. 36 48.

Pankaj Kumar Maskara (2006), "Participation of Investment Banks and Non-Bank Financial Institutions in Syndicated Loans", *available online: www.ssrn.org/papers.htm*

Penman Stephen, (2001), "Financial Statement Analysis and Security Valuation", McGraw-Hill Irwin, Second Edition, pp 66-545.

Planning Commission of India (1989), "Report of the Advisory Group on Consumer Industry", Ministry of Finance, Government of India, August

Rahman Shahidur, Tan Hwa Lian, Hew Lyn Ooi, Tan San Yih (2004), Identifying Financial Distress Indicators of Selected Banks in Asia", *Asian Economic Journal*, Vol. 18, 2004, No. IJ, pp. 45-51.

Ramasastri, A. S. and Unnikrishnan, N.K. (2006), "Is the Role of Banks as Financial Intermediaries Decreasing?", in *Economic and Political Weekly*, March 18th, pp.1063-1068.

Raj C Besant, (1989), "Corporate Financial Management–An Introduction", Tata McGraw-Hill Publishing Company Ltd, Second Edition, pp. 17-31,135-144.

Rangarajan, C., (2000), "Structural Reforms in Indian Banking and Finance: A Case Study of India" , Research and Information System for the Non Aligned and other Developing Countries (RIS) and Institute of South East Asian Studies (SEAS), Capital Publishing Company, New Delhi.

Reingnaum Marc (1992), " Revival of the Small-Firm Effect", *Journal of Portfolio Management*, Vol.18, No. 3 (Spring), pp. 55-62/

Reserve Bank of India , (2005), "Performance of Private Corporate Sector in the Post Liberalization Period", Reserve Bank of India Bulletin, November

Jay R.Ritter (2003), Economic Growth and Equity Returns, *available online:www.cba.ufi.edu*

Robinson, Marguerite S (2002), "The Micro-Finance Revolution, Vol. 2: Lessons from Indonesia"., The World Bank.

Roth A.V, Jackson III W.E (1995), "Strategic Determinants of Service Quality and Performance: Evidence from the Banking Industry", Management Science, 41, pp.1720-1733

Rousseau, P. L, P. Wachtel, (2000), "Equity Markets and Growth: Cross-Country Evidence on Timing and Outcomes: 1980-1995", *Journal of Banking and Finance*, 24,pp.1933-1957

Ross Levine, (2002), "Industry Growth and Capital Allocation: Does Having a Market-or Bank-Based System Matter?" *Journal of Financial Economics* pp. 60.

Saha Kausick, (2003), "Can the Ordinance Recover NPAs?", IIMB Management Review, March, pp. 19-27.

Sanyal Paroma, Shankar Rashmi, (2005), " Financial Sector Reforms and Bank Efficiency in India", *online: people.brandies.edu*, October, pp 2-31.

Saravanan,P, (2001), "A Study on Working Capital Management in Non-Banking Finance Companies", *Finance India*, Vol. 15, Part 3, pp. 987-994.

Saurina Jesus, Trucharte Carlos (2004), "The Impact of Basel II on Lending to Small–and Medium-Sized Firms: A Regulatory Policy Assessment Based on Spanish Credit Register Data", *Journal of Financial Services Research*, 26:2, pp.121-144.

Schmit Mathias, (2004), "Credit Risk in the Leasing Industry", Journal of Banking & Finance, Vol. 28, pp. 811-833.

Schwert, William, (1989), "Why does Stock Market Volatility Change over Time?", *Journal of Finance*, 44 (5), pp.1115–53

Seema Sagar,(1999), "Financial Performance of Leasing Companies, During the Quinquennium Ending 1989-90" Reserve Bank of India: Occasional Papers, Vol. 16, No. 3 September 95, pp. 223-236.

Sharma, S (2005), "Consumer Durable Financing." Federation of Indian Chambers of Commerce and Industry publications *(undated), www.ficci.com/ ficci/cmi/ cim15.htm*

Shawn Cole and Esther Duflo, (2004), "Banking Reform in India," in Bery, S. B. Bosworth and A. Panagariya, India Policy Forum, Volume 1. Washington, DC: National Council of Applied Economic Research; Brookings Institution, pp. 277-332

Shawn Cole and Esther Duflo,(2002), "Bank-based or Market-based Financial Systems: Which is Better?" *Journal of Financial Intermediation*, 11, pp.1-30.

Sherman H. David, Gold Franklin (1985), "Bank branch Operating Efficiency, DEA evaluation", Journal of Banking and Finance 9 (1985), Elvesier, pp. 297-315. North-Holland,

Shleifer, (2002), "The Regulation of Entry," Quarterly Journal of Economics, 117 (1), pp. 1-37.

Shibai Saturi (2004), "Assessing the Impact of Financial and Capital Market Reforms on Firms' Corporate Financing Patterns in India", *Article, Asia Economic Journal*, 5:2, pp.189-229.

Sinha Sanjay (2003), " Financial Services for Low Income Families: An Appraisal", Management Review, Indian Institute of Management, Bangalore, June 2003

Sinkey, Joseph F. Jr., Joseph Terza, and Robert Dince (1977), "Problem and Failed Banks, Bank Examinations and Early-Warning Systems: A Summary." Financial Crises. Edward I. Altman and Arnold W. Sametz, Editors. NewYork, NY: Wiley Interscience Inc.,1977.

Sinkey, J.F. (1992), "Commercial Bank Financial Management in the Financial Services Industry", Fourth edition New York: Maxwell Macmillan International Edition.

Sitaraman Krishnan, (2007), "RBI Guidelines for NBFCs to have no impact on Ratings of CRISIL rated NBFCs", CRISIL RatingScan, Feb, pp. 3-7.

Sitaraman Krishnan, (2007), "Will NBFCs Continue to have a Role? Innovation and Partnership: The Road Ahead", CRISIL RatingScan, Feb, pp 14-17.

Smith III, R L and Schweikart, J A (1992), "A Better Way to Assess Branch Profitability", *ABA Banking Journal*, Vol. 84, No. 4, pp.54-56.

Sodokin Koffi (2006), "Functional and Structural Complementarities of Banks and Micro Banks in L.D.Cs (Least Developed Countries)", November, *available online: www.ungaro.u-bourgogne.fr*, pp. 2-22.

Solomons D, (1965), "Divisional Performace: Measurement and Control", Homewood, Illinois, Irwin

Soterious A, Zenios S.A (1998), "Operations, Quality and Profitability in the Provision of Banking Services", *Management Science.*

Speed, R J (1991), "Marketing, Strategy and Performance in the UK Retail Financial Services Industry", Doctoral Thesis, Loughborough University of Technology.

Srinivasan. T.N (2003), "Indian Economic Reforms: A Stocktaking", Conference Proceedings, Annual Conference on Indian Economic Policy Reform, Yale University, June 2003, *available online: www.econ.yale.edu*

Stewart G.B (1991), "The quest for Value", Harper, New York

Stulz, Rene, (1999), "Globalization of Equity Markets and the Cost of Capital", Working Paper, National Bureau of Economic Research, UK, W.P. 7021, pp.2-70.

Stulz, Rene, (2005), "The Limits of Financial Globalization," (Presidential address) *Journal of Finance*, 60 (4), pp. 1595-1638.

Tarapore, S (1999), "Indian Banking: Preparing for the Next Round of Reforms., in India -A Financial Sector for the Twenty-First Century", J A Hanson and Sanjay Kathuria (editors), Oxford University Press.

Tate, T. (1998), "An Introduction to Modeling Outcomes in the Behavioral and Social Sciences", Boston, MA: Pearson Custom Publishing.

Taxmann, (2004), "Statutory Guide for Non-Banking Financial Companies", Taxmann Allied Services (P) Ltd, Revised Edition, pp. 1.2-7.3.

Tezel Ahmet (2003), "Return Measures and Firm's Performance: An Empirical Investigation, 1991-2000", August 2003 *available online: http://*207.36.165.114/Denver/Papers/Tezel1.pdf.

Thygerson, K J (1991), 'Modeling Branch Profitability', *Journal of Retail Banking,* Vol. 13, No.3, Fall, pp.19-24.

Thiyagarajan G, Arul Raj A, (2005), "The Strongest Link of Non-Banking Financial Institutions in the Financial Market", Conference on Research in Finance and Accounting, Paper Presented Indian Institute of Management, Lucknow, pp. 63-70.

Thiyagarajan G, Arul Raj A, (2005), "Weak hint between macroeconomic growth and earnings of Non-banking financial companies on India. Context," International Conference in Economics and Finance, 25-26th May 2005 University Malaysia Sabah, Malaysia.

Tirole, J, (1985), "Asset Bubbles and Overlapping Generations", Econometrica 53, pp. 1071–1100.

Treacy, W. and M. Carey, (2000), "Credit Rating Systems at large US Banks" Federal Reserve Bulletin, November 1998, and *Journal of Banking & Finance,* 24, 24, pp.167-201.

Ursel Baumann, Glenn Hoggarth and Darren Pain, (2005), "The Substitution of Bank for Non-bank Corporate Finance: Evidence for the United Kingdom", Working Paper, Bank of England, No. 274, July.

Van Horne, J C and Wachowicz, Jr J M (1995), "Fundamentals of Financial Management", 9th edn, Prentice Hall International, Inc., Englewood Cliffs, New Jersey.

Varma R Jayanth (1998), "Indian Financial Sector Reforms: A Corporate Perspective", *Vikalpa,* IIM Ahmedabad, Jan- Mar, Vol 23, No. 1, pp. 27-38.

Varma R Jayanth, (2001), "Indian Financial Sector after a Decade of Reforms", *available online: www.ccsindia.org,* pp. 1-37.

Vasudev C.M, (1998), "Report of the Task Force on Non-Banking Finance Companies", Gazette, Ministry of Finance, Government of India June 98.

Vemuti Somasekhar, (2007), "NBFCs Profitability under Pressure due to Competition", CRISIL RatingScan, Feb., pp. 8-13.

Vittas Dimitri, (1991), "Measuring Commercial Bank Efficiency: Use and Misuse of Bank Operating Ratios", Financial Policy and Systems, Working Papers, World Bank, November, pp. 1-49.

Whalen Gary, Thomson B James, (1988), "Using Financial Data to Identify changes in Bank Condition", *Review; Research,* Cleveland University, Q2, pp.2-26.

Van Horne, J C and Wachowicz, Jr J M (1995), "Fundamentals of Financial Management", 9th edn, Dryden Prentice.

Yadav, R.A., (1986), "Working Capital Management-A Parametric Approach", The Chartered Accountant , May, pp. 951-952.

Yap, C. (1997), "Users' Perceptions of the Need for Cash Flow Statements–Australian Evidence", *European Accounting Review,* 6(4): pp. 653-672.

You Hwan Tan (2005), "Indian Banking Sector Reforms: Reviews and Prospects", *International Area Review,* Vol. 8, No. 2, August, pp. 167-189

Yue Piyu, (1992), "Data Envelopment Analysis and Commercial Bank Performance: A Primer with Applications to Missouri Banks", *available online: www. research.stlouisfed.org,* pp. 31-39.

Zimmerman, J.L (1997), "EVA and Divisional Performance Measurement: Capturing Synergies and Other Issues", *Journal of Applied Corporate Finance,* 10(2), pp. 98-109.